LIVING LONGER, LIVING BETTER

John Baudhuin and Linda Hawks

WINSTON PRESS

Unless otherwise noted, all Bible quotations are from *The New English Bible,* © 1961, 1970 by the Delegates of the Oxford University Press and the Syndics of the Cambridge University Press. Reprinted by permission. Quotations marked NAB are taken from *The New American Bible,* © 1970 by the Confraternity of Christian Doctrine, Washington, D.C. Used by permission of the copyright owner. All rights reserved.

Grateful acknowledgment is made to Random House, Inc., for the excerpt from *The Prophet* by Kahlil Gibran.

This book was written as a project of the Senior Counseling Program, North Suburban Family Service Center, Coon Rapids, Minnesota. The program was made possible in part under the federal Older Americans Act through a grant from the Metropolitan Council Region XI Area Agency on Aging under an area plan approved by the Minnesota Board on Aging.

Cover design: Evans-Smith & Skubic

Library of Congress Catalog Card Number: 82-50291

ISBN: 0-86683-671-3

Printed in the United States of America.

5 4 3 2 1

Winston Press, Inc.
430 Oak Grove
Minneapolis, Minnesota 55403

This book is dedicated
to the living memory of
Evelyn Riste.

The Serenity Prayer

God, grant me the serenity
to accept the things I cannot change,
the courage to change the things I can,
and the wisdom to know the difference.

Acknowledgments

We feel we should acknowledge some of the people who helped in the conception and creation of this book. It began as a project of the Senior Counseling Program, North Suburban Family Service Center, Coon Rapids, Minnesota. Don Wegsheider, then the Director of Human Services for the City of Coon Rapids, Minnesota, had said in the spring of 1978 that the Senior Counseling Program should "write some kind of book" containing useful information about aging. Some concepts from his writing and that of Sharon Wegsheider provided a conceptual framework for the book. Elaine Vogt, a good friend, provided help and inspiration in addition to her highly skilled editorial ideas. Robert Sorg, with the Prudential Insurance Company, offered invaluable advice regarding financial opportunities. The Rev. Robert Harvey, an Episcopal priest with the Diocese of Minnesota, gave useful ideas on spiritual aspects of aging. Edith Sheldon, receptionist at the program, encouraged and inspired us as we brought the book to completion. We also thank all the senior citizens of Coon Rapids and the Anoka County, Minnesota, area for being patient and encouraging from start to finish. Finally, we salute and dedicate this book to perhaps our greatest friend, Evelyn Riste. She was famous for making the best cherry cheesecake in Anoka County, and for having the best and most sincere smile. She is not alive to see the completion of this work, but we are certain she is somewhere, criticizing, correcting, and loving us as much as she always did.

Contents

To Our Senior Friends

Some of you have been here for a very long time
Have watched the weather wear down the red
   sides of barns
And change them to the soft grays of late
   November

And others of you are new arrivals
Pushed sometimes from some past-filled house
   with large rooms
To a small square space in a cement tower

Most of you seem at peace and wish only
To have a good time, visit family and friends, and
   stay healthy
But some carry within a thousand tortures
And some are haunted by ghosts no one can fully
   understand
Still others are simply very tired, and very alone

You look at the late day and struggle for the
   courage to wait
And offer up your lives, yourselves, your wisdom,
We are at one with the rising of the sun and as
   sure
With its going down
We blaze together into the long night
With all the glory and certainty of the stars
We hand this to you now, imperfect, but a labor of
   love

From your love

We look upon your long labors
The still, gentle sculptures
Your faces make against the greening land
And we are proud

This is our small blessing and thanksgiving to you

—John Baudhuin

Introduction

"It was the best of times, it was the worst of times" begins *A Tale of Two Cities* by Charles Dickens. This fits well for those of us who are now in that great transition period of life which begins somewhere between the ages of fifty-five and sixty-five. Like it or not, we all emerge from that time senior citizens. This time of transition then, is truly a "tale of two cities" for many of us, because it is a journey from work to retirement, from children to grandchildren, and from busyness to sometimes long periods of unscheduled hours. It is truly a best and worst of times. Robert Butler, a nationally known gerontologist (one who specializes in the health care of the elderly), states that with increased health-care improvements and the elimination of the major killer diseases such as cancer and heart disease, most of us will be living longer and more healthful lives. Right now, approximately twenty million Americans are sixty-five years and older. That's about 10% of the population. By 2020 A.D., this could increase to 25%. Many estimate that, without accidents or diseases, we could all live to be ninety or one hundred years of age. With better transportation systems, more housing opportunities, improved health care, and other favorable legislation for senior citizens, this can be truly a "best time."

Then too, this particular generation of older citizens is one which is unique in world history. Never

before has there been a group of people who have
been through so much in one lifetime. This is best
emphasized by some artifacts in the office of Con-
gressman Claude Pepper in Washington, D.C. He
reportedly has on his wall a memento signed by
Orville and Wilbur Wright, the two men who made
the first human flight of a powered aircraft in 1903.
On another wall, he has a memento signed by Neil
Armstrong, the first human being to walk upon the
surface of our moon. The generation of seniors has
seen a great deal, has a great deal to remember and
a great deal to teach. We personally hold a special
regard for those incidents and recollections that have
been shared with us. Senior citizens are giving back
to Americans our history, or if you will, our roots.

Yet Robert Butler asks the ultimate question about
old age in America in his book *Why Survive?*. Here
he documents the vast number of health problems,
economic problems, social problems, and mental
health problems that seem to plague older persons
in our society. Statistics generally indicate that 80%
of all persons over sixty-five have some kind of serious health problem. Estimates which vary somewhat state that one-fourth to one-half of the older
population lives below the poverty level. Medicare
helps, but in many cases covers less than half the
person's medical expenses. One illness can wipe out
a life's work in a few weeks or months. Over one-
fourth of all seniors reportedly live in substandard
housing. Millions of older persons may need atten-
tion for depression and other mental health prob-

lems, problems often brought on in part by the kinds of stress mentioned above. Statistics show alarming rates of alcoholism and *rising rates of addiction* to prescription medications among seniors. At least 25% of known suicides are committed by persons age sixty-five and older, a rate two and one-half times that of the general population. The statistics go on, and we find more reasons to ask, "Why survive?" "Why bother, if it is going to be like this?" Indeed, how many of us have heard someone say, "Why, when I hit sixty-five, I hope someone just takes me out and shoots me"?

Why survive? First, because life itself often has surprises and unexpected gifts around the next corner which make the whole adventure worthwhile. We believe life is more than a mere chemical and biological accident. It is a special and sacred gift of God, and each person is a special and unique individual whose worth is important to the scheme of things. We also believe that life is more than mere existence or survival. Why survive? We survive the bad times; we exist through the long and lonely times, so that we might truly live. Good living, as most of us have learned by now, is not solely dependent on wealth and health. We live best in wholeness—when we feel complete as a person. In this book, we will talk a great deal about being a whole person, that is, being able to live as fully and happily as possible. The purpose of this book, then, is to answer the question "Why survive?" and to offer some suggestions as to how we might live a life of wholeness. The ideas are drawn from our experience, your experience, and the experience of others within and outside the helping professions. This is intended to be a reference book, to be read in bits and pieces if you wish, or all at once. Take from it what you wish, and leave the rest.

1

The Whole-Person Concept

Wholeness. At first this word might summon up visions of those whose work in life is completed, who have found all the answers and filled in all the blanks and can at last rest assured that they have made their contribution to the world. But as John Newman wisely noted, "Growth is the only evidence of life." In keeping with this idea, we view the concept of the whole person as one not of being finished, but of continually growing and striving to maintain a harmony or sense of balance so that no one facet of our being overshadows the rest.

The artist Pablo Picasso once said, when asked why his later paintings were so much more daring than his early ones, "Madame, it takes a long time to become young." We believe that it also takes a long time for many persons to realize their own powers and rights as human beings. We all have six kinds of power available to draw upon in our attempt to continue growing. But we must first become aware of them and then begin to nurture them as life-altering powers. Ultimately, the strength and balance of these powers will determine how we feel about ourselves and our future and how well we shape and enrich our lives.

Perhaps the most central power in our lives is spiritual. For many people this may be nurtured by a religious faith—a means of strength and clarity in their lives. For others, this spiritual power may be sustained by a philosophy or some central life-principle. Whatever gives purpose and meaning to our lives nourishes our spiritual power.

A second important resource is our mental power. This is the ability to grow, to change, to integrate the many aspects of our lives into a functioning whole. With the approach of our senior years, this ability becomes increasingly important, because the changes in our lives become greater and more numerous. Our mental power helps us to prepare for many of these changes, to adapt to some others, and to learn new things, so that in our senior years we may develop a different and often better style of life.

Our social power consists mainly of our ability to establish and maintain meaningful relationships with other people. This can be vitally important at a time of life when we may be losing friends and loved ones because of retirement, a change in residence, or death. Reaching out to other people with friendship and love can play a significant role in making our lives worth living.

The physical aspect of our lives involves the power we may develop through the use of our bodies, our skills, and our sexuality. Aging is often associated with a marked decline in these areas, but with understanding and respectful use of our bodies, we can maintain and enjoy our physical powers well into old age.

The freedom to experience and express feelings is called our emotional power. This power really involves being in touch with ourselves and what we are feeling, so that we may express our feelings appropriately. Finally, all of us need to be aware of the power we have to make choices in our lives. This involves accepting responsibility for ourselves and our actions and choosing to accept the reality of a given situation. Being aware of our choices also requires that we know there are some circumstances over which we have power and some we must accept because we are powerless over them. As the Serenity Prayer states, it sometimes takes "wisdom to know the difference."

These are the main types of power in each of our lives. They may change in strength and balance as our lives change. But generally, we have the power to encourage the development of any or all of these powers and to bring them into harmony with each other for their most effective use in improving our lives.

2

Spiritual Power

Our spiritual power is at the base of everything else that makes us a whole person. It is the most important of all the person powers, yet often the least understood. Our greatest problem is our tendency to limit or confine spirituality to one area. For example, many of us tend to see religion and spirituality as one and the same thing. While matters religious are certainly matters spiritual as well, spirituality cannot be limited or contained, even by religion itself. Practicing a religion is perhaps our most earnest attempt to attain spirituality, but even religion does not fully contain it. Spirituality is unlimited; it contains all aspects of life and the universe itself. Thus we can be a spiritual person through our own particular religion or through some other means as well.

Victor Frankl, who was a concentration camp inmate during World War II, discovered that those who survived best were those who found some kind of meaning and purpose. In his book *Man's Search for Meaning* he shows that some inmates did this through their religion. An embrace from a long lost friend or relative, a new day, or even the end of an old day, can be just as meaningful and spiritual as a religious event. Many of us have learned over the years that a person's particular denomination or sect is not nearly as important as how the person applies his or her beliefs to everyday living.

There are many roadblocks to a healthy spiritual life. Perhaps the greatest spiritual problem or sin, if you will, is that of pride. The ancient Greeks called this *hubris,* the sin of excess. The theological definition of sin is "separation from God." It is excessive or false pride, the mistaken sense that we can do it all alone, that separates us from the love and care of God.

A British monk named Pelagius saw the great moral decline in Rome during the early days of the Church and was greatly shocked by it. The mistake that Pelagius made was to believe that somehow, by our efforts alone, we could overcome the evil within us and be better persons. This is the great heresy of Pelagianism. The modern version of that, familiar to many of us, is the so-called "self-made man." Many of us grew up believing that we must "pull ourselves up by our own bootstraps." Yet all major religions in the world teach us that on our own, despite our best intentions, we can't do it. The results of pride and the "I don't need anyone" attitude, evident in the Garden of Eden, were a separation from God that could be mended only by God, not by humans. St. Paul, a man of strong will and determination, wrote that in spite of all his "will to do good," "the good which I want to do, I fail to do; but what I do is the wrong which is against my will" (Romans 7:19).

An important aspect of spirituality is recognizing our need for others and for God as we understand

God. Pride in our work, our city, our family, and our nation are all good things and lead to a job done well. However, a false pride in a puffed-up self leads, as Scripture says, to a great fall. This is difficult for many of us to accept, since we may have been taught that we should never reveal a need for help or a need for others. Yet our greatest models, such as our friend the late Senator Hubert Humphrey, are those men who have the strength to let others know their feelings and their needs for others. Humphrey's openly tearful final address to Congress will not soon be forgotten.

Another great spiritual problem is that sometimes we become involved in religiosity rather than religion. We are all familiar with the person who answers every question with a quote from Scripture but who constantly points a finger at others. This person is often sincere and deeply convinced in his or her own beliefs, but religion and judgmental behavior can sometimes be used as a defense against life rather than as a means to a more fulfilled life.

God, we believe, comes to us through other people as well as directly, and a really spiritual person is open to people as well as to God. None of us is perfect; if we judge others, we will turn people away and find ourselves quite alone. Jesus said, "Why do you look at the speck of sawdust in your brother's eye, with never a thought for the great plank in your own?" (Matthew 7:3).

We think religion has a great deal to offer and can be a deciding factor in our longevity. One of the most

important things we have learned over the years is
the value of moderation and balance. Here are some
ideas that may help you find and use your spiritual
powers.

1. Be open to new views and concepts. Our tradi-
   tions and customs hold a great deal of meaning
   and comfort, but we need to remember that spirituality is always open to growth and change.
2. Feel free to return to earlier religious practices if
   this is comfortable. Many of us have left behind
   earlier religious or spiritual pursuits and may feel
   embarrassed about returning to a church or syn-
   agogue after many months or years of absence.
   Remember that the greatest message of any religion should be that of understanding and for-
   giveness but above all, welcome.
3. Maintain regular spiritual pursuits, such as daily
   readings of inspirational, spiritual, or religious literature, and daily prayer and meditation. Also, a
   regular time for reflection or meditation can help
   make sense out of the day and bring meaning and
   serenity to our lives. Prayer can be as simple as
   merely *talking,* and meditation can be simply *listening.* We have a great deal to say, and there is
   much to which we can listen.
4. Refrain from judging the beliefs and practices of
   others. Consider the tragedies, such as those in
   northern Ireland or Iran, that occur because of
   intolerance. Persons with a healthy spirituality can
   embrace all people while maintaining their own
   identity.

5. Be active. Many feel that after a certain age, they should no longer be a voice in church or religious activities. Actually, some of the finest ministry is done by persons who have the experience and the time to share with others.

3

Mental Power

Mental Power and Aging

We all have mental power. In fact, it is our mental power that separates us from all other creatures. Unfortunately, we have tended to define mental power by trying to measure a person's basic intelligence or IQ. Sometimes we also use such yardsticks as years of education, degrees, and professional or business standing. Those of us without such qualifications, like the scarecrow in *The Wizard of Oz*, tend to put ourselves down. Many of us, because of the hard times during the Depression, or perhaps for other understandable reasons, simply did not have the educational opportunities that people have today. Yet we all learn. In fact, research shows that we are constantly learning and growing throughout our entire lives. Studies show, for example, that our vocabulary constantly grows all through life. If, then, we have a limited formal education but many years in that "graduate school" known as life, we may be wiser than we think.

A common misunderstanding about aging is that as we get older we inevitably become more confused and strange until we reach that greatly feared condition known as senility. Indeed, some older persons do appear to have this condition. It is now thought, however, that becoming senile is not necessarily a condition we must all face as we get older. Research shows that often causes other than age are at work and that so-called "senility" is frequently reversible. One study guesses that up to a million older Americans diagnosed as "senile" may simply be overmedicated. (See the material in "Medication" in Chapter 5.) Most of us are likely to remain mentally alert for the total span of our days, for our mental powers are meant to grow rather than decline. This means that we have not only the right but the responsibility to make decisions for ourselves, to investigate all sides of questions that affect us. We even have the right to change our minds! In defense of that, Ralph Waldo Emerson said, "A foolish consistency is the hobgoblin of little minds."

Education

We should remember that it is never too late to learn. And today many opportunities for formal education are available to older persons. All over the country, institutions of higher learning offer older persons the opportunity to audit a college course for a very small fee. Also, many communities sponsor interesting and useful courses for adults through their local school systems. A good friend, for example, recently retired from a lifelong career as a carpenter to take a two-year training course in a new field. This person *started* a second career as a counselor at age sixty-four. Stories of grandmothers and even great-grandmothers getting their high school diplomas or college degrees are no longer a curiosity. New federal requirements are gradually making most institutions accessible to those with physical disabilities. The time has never been better for older persons to hit the books.

Seniors themselves are another important source of education. Many have hidden talents, skills, and experiences that are not found in books. During our years as counselors to seniors, we spent a great deal of time discovering the vast wealth of knowledge many seniors have within them. For example, one senior we knew took wild animals into classrooms and taught children about animal survival, ecology, and conservation. Another senior used his experience as a choir director to organize Christmas programs for the seniors in his building. And finally, a woman who had worked many years as a writer and editor gave us invaluable help in the writing of this book.

Education, then, is available to us in more ways than ever. Many libraries, for instance, carry large-print editions of popular and classic works for those with limited eyesight. Many senior clubs offer new experiences that are both fun and educational. Churches and community centers fill their schedules with classes, tours, seminars, and workshops. Education is not memorizing; rather it is remembering in a meaningful and constructive way. It is a treasure of knowledge and a gift beyond all gifts to share with others. Those of us survive best who have wide and varied interests and can seldom journey through a day without having heard or observed something new. The Preacher Qoheleth wrote "there is nothing new under the sun" (Ecclesiastes 1:9). Yet that next undiscovered thing is always new when we first come upon it.

Change

We are always changing, and major changes can be difficult for anyone. A small child will go to war over the loss of a favorite blanket or toy; a parent will go into spells of anxiety over a first date, a first car, the marriage and moving away of a son or daughter. Most of us are dealing with change all our lives. Yet, save for the first few years of life, no years are so filled with change as are the sixties. That decade is often the time of retirement, grandchildren who are no longer children, moving to a smaller house, or giving up the lake cottage. It can be a time of great losses—the loss of a spouse, parents, brothers and sisters, or good friends.

Those who can cope with change best are those whose lives are founded on a deeply spiritual base, who are able to make new friends and try new activities, and who are also able to both laugh and cry openly without feeling these are wrong. But no one likes constant major changes. Because of change, we need to find new meanings and new directions. Sometimes we need the help of friends, relatives, ministers, and counselors to find these new directions. We should not feel ashamed or guilty about needing help.

Most persons react to change at first with disbelief, then a sense of depression, then perhaps some confusion, and finally, a sense of new beginnings. The lesson of most religions is that even at the darkest times, the seeds of new beginnings are present. God, it is said, is full of surprises. Biblical stories such as the miracle at the Red Sea, the empty tomb, and the upper room illustrate the nature of change and the opportunities that lie therein. The changes we experience may ultimately be pleasant but will not be totally so, for the deep hurt of grief will always be with us in some ways. Yet we can go on even though everything appears to be falling down around us, and we can perhaps even gain some useful insights as we go. We need to view the changes we go through as challenges, and, as difficult as it may seem, perhaps even as opportunities for growth.

The Dance of Change

The moon is full
having followed its cycle
to fruition.
The tide recedes
and then again
rushes, rushes to the shore.
As I measure the beach
with bare feet on cold, wet sand
and with a night wind in my hair,
I see once more the cycles of my life,
turning against the darkened sky.

The child I was,
who begat the girl, begat the woman
that I was, and the woman that I am
begat the child.
The love that was
then turned to loss,
which turned to pain,
and then to grief,
which turned to strength,
which gave birth to love.
For pain I think is no stranger
to birthing.
And the clear-eyed child-wisdom
then turned to hunger,
which reached for knowledge,
and turned to passion
that burned for truth

and life and love
and clear-eyed wisdom.

For all my days
have been a dance of change
and bare feet
on cold, wet beaches
washed by the tide—
always changing, always the same,
always growing,
and always, always
alive and new.

—Linda Hawks
9/15/78

4

Social Power

Give your hearts, but not into each other's keeping. For only the hand of life can contain your hearts. And stand together yet not too near together: For the pillars of the temple stand apart, and the oak tree and the cypress grow not in each other's shadow.

— Kahlil Gibran, *The Prophet*

Relationships

How we view ourselves as individuals has a great deal to do with how we relate to other people, whether they are friends, family, or those most dear to us. All of us—man or woman, child or adult—have a need for both separateness or independence and intimacy. We can see these needs clearly acted out by the small child who one moment will say "Please don't help me anymore," and the next moment will be reaching out to mother for comforting because of a scraped knee. Although we may express these needs very differently, we do carry them with us into our adulthood.

Intimacy is that feeling of being close to and safe with someone because we know we are totally accepted by that person. No matter how vulnerable we make ourselves to this other person, we trust that our openness will not be used against us. Sometimes this closeness may be expressed physically, but often it finds expression in other ways such as long talks or shared experiences. Intimacy is a very rich part of life, but it is not all of life. Years of marriage or of friendship must have spaces for the times of closeness to remain meaningful. Nearly all creative work requires a degree of alone time for concentrated thought and planning. But aloneness (or a quiet time in a group) is not to be confused with loneliness, which is involuntary isolation from others.

Intimacy and separateness complement each other. Just as it is impossible to applaud loudly if we move our hands only an inch apart, it is impossible to enjoy true intimacy with another person if we do not allow ourselves a time of separateness and independence. Then our coming together can be bright and real and enthusiastic—like true applause.

Independence and separateness are very frightening ideas for many of us because they conjure up visions of loneliness. But this need not be the case. Being separate or independent for awhile does not mean that we must be that way indefinitely. Separateness can be an opportunity to find out who we are and what we have to offer. It allows us a breathing space in which to grow. And it can make our times of intimacy that much more meaningful.

Stages of a Relationship

Love, friendship, marriage—these are all examples of relationships we may have with one another. They involve varying degrees of intimacy, yet these and other close relationships go through some common phases.

When a couple begins a relationship, they often become completely engrossed in it. It is a time of discovering the many wonderful ways in which the two are alike, the interests they share, and also the many enjoyable ways in which they differ and complement each other. It is rather like seeing one's own reflection in someone else.

No one can say exactly how long that first rose-colored time will last. But it will end, and eventually the persons involved must try to integrate their respective values and habits, or else they will remain divided by their differences. He may love the outdoors, while she is a dedicated city person. She may be a "night person" and he a "day person"; or one of them may eat crackers in bed. This awakening nearly always leads to disappointment in both partners.

It may be difficult for two persons to reconcile these differences. Each may wonder why he or she chose this partner in the first place. A real danger here is that one or both will use confidences shared in happier days to hurt the other person. Such a strategy can destroy trust and create mutual disapproval.

Usually about this time the two realize that the relationship will not fill all their needs. It does not seem to matter that their expectations are not very realistic. Following disappointment, resentment often creeps into the picture as each partner silently charges the other with failure to love: "If you *really* loved me, you would *know* what to do." And since they are not mind readers they may end up feeling rejected and helpless. These unsatisfied needs can totally eclipse the possibility of future happiness. Sexual difficulties are likely to appear, for physical intimacy becomes nearly impossible in an atmosphere of rejection.

It is important at this point to remember that there is a variety of choices that a partner can make about how to relate to that other person. A counselor may help one become more aware of what the choices are in a situation like this.

Many relationships never reach the third stage—acceptance—either because the partners give up or because they cannot, for whatever reasons, progress past the anger and frustration of the second stage. But it is possible during this time to balance expectations with reality. The extremes of romance and discord can be changed into understanding and lasting affection if both partners are truly interested in preserving the relationship.

But even to begin the process of changing the negative to the positive, both partners must share at least some essential attitudes: a mutual attraction, an acknowledgment of the other's worth, a willingness to give as well as take, and perseverance. Only an open frame of mind will allow the partners to see that they must change their feelings as well as their behavior toward one another.

This is a large undertaking, and so the two must be open to learning several new approaches and skills.

- They must be ready to acknowledge their own vulnerability and that of their partner.
- They must begin to assume responsibility for their own emotions and avoid hiding or projecting them onto their partner.
- They must try to gain a clear understanding of their own needs and of the defenses they use to keep from being hurt.
- They must learn the importance of getting in tune with their own feelings.

A combination of realism, personal responsibility, and a sincere desire to keep the relationship intact can lead to a healthy balance between independence and dependence on each other. On the way to attaining this balance the partners should be able to look each other straight in the eyes and to say, "Here I am. I am letting you see me as I really am. I am human—sometimes strong, sometimes weak and with many faults. I feel that you are letting me see you in the same way. I accept you as I hope you will accept me. I find you beautiful in your humanity. And though we are different, I believe that we can make something beautiful and lasting together, and I am committed to working together with you to make that happen."

Achieving this level of acceptance and commitment is not something that happens automatically in any relationship, though reaching it may be easier for some than for others. In many relationships it is never reached at all. And even once it has been reached, changes in the people involved or in their life situations may bring about another time of discovering new differences and dissatisfactions. This sometimes occurs in a marriage when children leave home or when one or both partners retire and significantly change their life-style. But when two people can not only survive together but come to appreciate their differences and disappointments and reach a time of accepting and being accepted, of caring and being cared for, the reward is one of the things that makes life worth living.

Maintaining Relationships

The most important part of maintaining relationships is that often-repeated word, "communication." How well we communicate is the key to whether or not we will maintain relationships that are both rewarding and meaningful. Those whose lives are interwoven with others' in a close yet comfortable fashion seem to be the happiest people. The trick is to recognize when we need to be close to others and when we need some time of separation. Our solar system is a good example of relationships. Should the planets go too fast, they would leave the orbit around the sun and be lost in space. On the other hand, if the planets went too slowly, they would soon be swallowed up into the sun. Like the planets, each of us has a greater or lesser need to be close. We have our own "boundaries" through which we allow only a few to pass. Some like people very close; others want more distance. In a good relationship, we respect this need for distance as well as the desire for closeness. The best marriages usually are the result of many decades of this sort of give-and-take as two people define their limits and explore each other's boundaries.

There are several levels of relationships. First is the casual acquaintance. This is someone we meet once, in the left-field bleachers at the game, on the bus, or at a dance. Then there are associates, people we meet while involved in another activity, such as work, a church project, or a political campaign. And there are friends. These are people we do things with beyond the work situation, people whom we seek out and want to be with. Finally, there are close friends, and people we might call companions, people with whom we would share anything, to whom we would give anything, and for whom we might be willing to lay down our very lives. Most people have only a few such companions in their entire lives. Relatives, as we know, may be at any of the levels of relationship which have been mentioned. Often, but not always, a spouse will be considered a companion, or someone closer to us than anyone else.

As we reach the sixties and seventies, many relationships have been disrupted by death, illness, or
moving. It is sometimes difficult to form new relationships at that time of life. Realistically, we are
aware that we may never have another relationship
as close as one we may have had with a spouse,
relative, or lifelong friend. Once again, the rules for
good communication enter in. These rules for communication can be remembered by the word HOW.
We should try to communicate with *honesty, openness,* and *willingness. Honesty* means being direct
and stating exactly what we mean, sometimes even
at the risk of offending the other person. Dishonesty
in communication is easily detected, even by small
children. *Openness* means that we are willing to share
ourselves, and that we are willing to listen to the
sharing of others, even if it does not exactly agree
with our way of thinking. *Willingness* means the
intention to go more than just halfway to meet that
other person. Willingness is that ability mentioned
in the New Testament to go the extra mile with
another person. No deep relationship will survive
merely on a 50-50 basis. Rather, both parties must
do all they can to make it work.

A final word about relationships: There are many
places now where older persons can get together
for social and other activities. It is not within the
scope of this book to list them all, so for particulars
we suggest calling your nearest senior citizen group
or agency. Basically, three or four general kinds of
activities are available: First, there are senior citi-

zens' clubs, where people get together often for social activities such as trips, dances, parties, cards, and so on. Second, programs such as congregate dining are within reach of most people, and transportation is often provided. At a congregate dining site, people will gather at noon for a hot meal, socializing, and often some sort of entertainment. Those who wish may donate a small amount, for there are no fees. Third, there are volunteer organizations that provide seniors with opportunities to help in nursing homes, social service agencies, schools, hospitals, and daycare centers. A program such as RSVP (Retired Seniors Volunteer Program) is an excellent example. Finally, a major source of activity for seniors is local churches. Also, there are many "senior citizen discounts" offered at concerts, sporting events, beauty salons, co-ops, movies, and other attractions. The local senior group can usually provide names of places that offer such discounts.

Relationships are part of who we are and should be carefully nurtured. They reinforce our humanity and make life worthwhile by involving us in situations that require a degree of feeling and caring. Our systems require this stimulation in order to feel alive. We need to have the occasions of empathy, sympathy, grief, pain, loss, beauty, laughter, and joy— the whole range of human emotion—to maintain interest in living.

Lastly, two important relationships that have not been mentioned are the relationship with self and the relationship we have with a Power greater than ourselves. The section on spiritual power deals more fully with these. It is our hope that some of these guidelines may help in all of our relationships, for they are all important. As the writer of Genesis said, we are not meant to be alone.

5
Physical Power

I give you thanks that I am fearfully, wonderfully made.
—Psalm 139:14, *NAB*

Physical Needs

Our physical powers are very closely related to our other person powers. In fact, ancient Hebrew prophets and sages spoke of the unity of the body and soul. They believed that if the physical self was affected, so was the spiritual self. Most doctors today believe there is a strong relationship between physical illness and depression. Many Greek philosophers, however, believed that the body and the spiritual self were separate entities; and they tended to hold that the spiritual self was superior to the physical. Some early Christians believed this as well, and for many centuries, Western philosophy taught that the intellect was superior to the emotional self, the soul superior to the body. This may in part explain the tendency of Westerners to neglect and even downgrade the physical self. Many of us were taught from an early age that our physical self was almost an unfortunate necessity. Yet Hebrew and Christian thought teaches that we are to care for our bodies because they are as much a part of the gift of creation

as are our minds. Tragically, many of us do not realize this until we have neglected our physical selves.
In this part of the book, we hope to explain some
facts and ideas that may help us in the maintenance
of what remains the most amazing machine in existence—the human body.

Biological Aspects of Aging

One undeniable fact about life is that we all age and
eventually die. It is very important to accept the fact
of our aging and death. However, this does not mean
that we should morbidly submit to the inevitable.
Aging is only another part of the process of being a
human being. Other cultures in other times often
viewed aging as some kind of illness to be shunned,
rather than as a natural process. Many tend to think
that nothing happens in aging, that we can be as
young at sixty as at thirty. This also is not true. The
answer lies somewhere between the extremes. Yes,
we do slow down and lose some of our physical ability
as we age. These losses are not a sign that we are
becoming worthless. If we are aware of some of the
changes that come with aging, we can prepare, as
in the Serenity Prayer, "to change the things we
can, and to accept the things we cannot change."
We cannot stop the years, but we can deal with them
effectively.

We actually begin to age, as we know it, from
about the age of thirty. Those who follow professional sports know only too well that after this time,

physical abilities deteriorate. The "Grand Old Man" of football, George Blanda, was well known because he was an active player well into his forties. Our peak physical abilities, then, go downhill by thirty, but we retain much of our ability many years beyond that point. We also retain our basic skills. So even though we may not be as strong, we are still as capable—often more capable—in later years.

In addition to a loss of muscular strength, we experience a gradual loss of resilience. Again, this varies with the individual, and it depends on the amount of exercise we get and the way we take care of ourselves.

Our body's systems also decline as we get older. Most people experience some decline of the senses. Hearing may begin to lose its sharpness in the late twenties, and vision loss can show up in the thirties. Possibly one out of four persons over sixty-five has a serious vision loss, and one out of five has a hearing problem. Most of us lose our sharpness of taste and smell to some extent. Our bones lose calcium, an important mineral for keeping them solid. The bone degeneration that may follow is known as osteoporosis. As joints in fingers, arms, and legs wear, some of us will experience inflammation and pain of the joints, known as arthritis. As joints "wear out," calcium deposits form, stiffening and sometimes crippling them. This wearing out kind of arthritis is known as osteo-arthritis. Also, our hearts reduce their output and are more likely to become diseased. The lungs lose some of their ability to expand and contract, and eventually some lungs may have only 50% of their previous capacity. The kidneys slow down in filtering the fluids of our systems, and the liver becomes smaller. As we age, we may become more susceptible to the latest virus or "bug" going around. Even our sleep patterns change: We tend to sleep less deeply and wake up more easily. Sleep changes are usually a perfectly normal aspect of aging.

Well, enough of the bad news. The good news is that most of us handle all the above changes with surprising calm and fortitude. Those most victimized by the aging process are perhaps those who attach too much importance to physical ability and appearance. While those things are certainly important, we know that a whole person is more than a physical self.

There are some ways of lessening the effects of aging so that the later years can not only be comfortable but enjoyable. There are two basic strategies for dealing with aging: The first is to live and care for ourselves in such a way as to prevent problems from arising. But we must also learn effective ways of coping with the problems that do arise, for over 80% of us over sixty-five have some health problems. Following are some ideas about prevention and coping that both seniors and doctors have taught us.

The two most important aspects of prevention are a balanced diet and moderate activity. Studies show that these are the real secrets to health and long life. Nutrition is our first line of defense against any physical or emotional problems. No food or chemical will prevent aging or fend off every illness, but good nutrition will make the aging process more graceful and the recovery from illness more swift and complete.

No matter how we rationalize, we all know that smoking is one of the most harmful things we can do to our lungs and circulatory system. Studies now show that smoking also harms those near the smoker. So if we do smoke, we should be careful to respect the rights of others to have a smoke-free atmosphere. We should be especially mindful of this as we get older, since our lung capacity gets smaller, and respiratory problems are a major killer of older persons. We should be very careful about what medicines and drugs we use. We have included near the end of this section a list of guidelines for the use of medicine and drugs. We should use alcoholic beverages in moderation only. It is known that alcohol causes severe damage to the liver and nervous system if used improperly, and the untold story of the emotional harm alcoholics do to themselves and their loved ones could fill many volumes. Alcoholism is at least as common among older persons as among any other given age group. Since it is an illness, any person, of any background and social situation, can become alcoholic. More information on this subject is available in the section on Emotional Power.

Activity is the other major aspect of prevention. Any sort of physical activity is better than none. Simple activities such as walking and swimming, for example, can be very helpful in keeping muscles strong and resilient. The slogan, "Use it or lose it" applies to our physical selves. Activity also means being involved with others. Statistics are beginning to reveal that there is a strong relationship between being active and staying well physically and emotionally. So the choice is ours. We can use it or lose it. (See the section on Fitness and Flexibility.)

Another good means of prevention is a regular visit to the doctor. A yearly physical is a good idea, and more frequent visits are necessary if there are definite problems. A health maintenance program may be available for this purpose in your area. A final idea for prevention of health problems is simply good self-care. Good personal hygiene and proper rest can work wonders. It is helpful to use a mirror after meals to check on one's teeth and general appearance. And it is a good idea to dress appropriately for the situations at hand. Sometimes it becomes too easy to spend the day or most of it in a robe or housecoat. Being active means getting out and meeting the challenge of a new day.

All the above practices help to prevent some health problems from occurring. They are all simple ideas that can become part of our daily habits for happiness and survival. In spite of good habits, we may develop some health problems anyway. Once again, coping becomes important. We begin to cope when we first admit the problem and finally come to accept it. To accept a problem does not mean we must like it: It only means that we recognize it and are willing to go on in spite of it. We will not give the problem power over our lives.

Diabetes is a common problem among older persons. (It can also strike the very young.) Diabetes is not now curable, but medical research has made it very treatable. Daily sugar checks, proper diet and rest, and the proper use of medication can usually control diabetes. It is also a good idea to take good care of hands and feet and to have regular eye examinations, since these areas become more vulnerable in diabetes. Walking and other exercise stimulates the natural production of insulin, so ask your doctor about a suitable regimen of physical activity of this sort. (Wearing a medical identification bracelet or tag is a good idea when one has diabetes.)

Arthritis is a very painful condition, particularly in northern or very humid areas. Again, "Use it or lose it" applies here. Moderate use of stiffening joints can sometimes help prevent them from becoming immobile. Some medications may help, but these should always be taken carefully and under a doctor's advice. Some arthritics have ulcers caused by excessive use of aspirin for pain. Arthritics run a great risk of becoming dependent on stronger pain measures, so a part of coping with arthritis may mean learning to live with some pain. Many people have learned to do this. There are also pain clinics available to teach people how to deal with chronic pain through non-chemical means. Then, too, the presence of others in our lives can go a long way to lessen pain. Pain is often more intense when we feel alone.

Many of us live in great fear of having a stroke. A stroke is actually a kind of brain injury that occurs when something goes wrong in the blood vessels leading to the brain. A stroke that injures one side of the brain will affect the opposite side of the body. For example, if a person's left half of the brain is injured, then there may be paralysis on the right side, and the speech will be affected. Persons can and often do recover very well from a stroke. Surgery, speech therapy, and physical therapy have often worked miracles. But unfortunately, not all will recover completely, and once again acceptance is important. The greatest improvement usually happens in the first few months or year, although in some cases, improvement will continue long beyond that. It is important to remember that someone whose speech has been affected can often understand clearly, and some will learn other ways of communicating. The person is not retarded or mentally slow just because he or she is simply no longer able to speak.

A final word about healing: If we examine most sacred writings, be they Christian, Hebrew, or some other faith, we will see that healing is also a spiritual activity. It is our belief that spirituality can have a great effect on physical healing. "Faith healing" and the like should be viewed with understandable caution, but we know that if people have a sense of meaning, purpose, and direction in their lives, they do tend to get sick less and heal faster. Cultivating our spirituality, then, is an important part of both prevention and coping. Spirituality is at the center of the whole-person powers. Knowing that all of nature is "on our side" throughout life and that the mind and body yearn after health until the very end helps to keep an optimistic attitude that makes for greater happiness. It is difficult to be utterly negative and forlorn when we are aware of this inner power.

Nutrition

Probably no other aspect of health maintenance is as important as nutrition. Ironically, however, nutrition is one area of health maintenance about which we still know relatively little. Until very recently, most medical schools taught very little about this subject. Now we find ourselves buried in an avalanche of diet books, exercise books, books for or against a particular food substance, and so forth. Most of these books contain at least *some* good insights about nutrition and diet. No one approach or fad diet is appropriate for everybody. Also, as our life-styles change, so should our nutritional habits. In discussing the subject of nutrition, we realize that we can at best offer only some general suggestions on the subject. For specific suggestions, a local nutritionist, your doctor, or a public health nurse can be very helpful. Pamphlets on the subject are available through health agencies and congregate dining sites.

The best single guideline for good nutrition comes from the ancient Greeks, who said that the greatest wrong was that of *hubris,* sometimes called the "sin of excess." Too much of even a good thing is not good. As we get older and family members move away, we may find ourselves cooking for only one or two persons. It becomes easy to use the convenience foods or not to cook at all. While our systems need fewer calories as we get older, we still need a good balance of foods to maintain the proper amounts of vitamins and minerals. It is commonly known that poor nutrition can make us more likely to pick up the latest virus or flu. Poor nutrition is a contributing factor in many more serious problems as well. Studies now show that some so-called "senile" patients in hospitals and nursing homes may have become this way partly because of poor nutrition. A deficiency of potassium can lead to very serious heart problems. A deficiency of calcium may be part of what causes osteoporosis, the gradual loss of minerals in our bones. With osteoporosis, bones become more brittle and we are more likely to break a leg or hip. And the list of problems caused by poor nutrition could go on and on.

What many may do after hearing of nutritional problems like the above is rush to the nearest pharmacy to buy vitamins and minerals. Actually, the best method of prevention is to have a well-balanced diet. A good diet will include fruits, vegetables, meat, fish, eggs, bread, high-fiber foods such as bran, and a *few* of the "goodies" as well. It is smart to avoid fats, refined sugar, excess salt and starches. The average meal at a congregate dining site, for example, includes at least one-third of our daily dietary requirements, and often more. We think it is best to have at least one complete meal a day, such as is served in congregate dining rooms. It seems easier to snack on starchy, less nutritious foods, but they may lead to serious problems without our even being aware of it. Since we are often cooking for just one or two, it is a good idea to make a full recipe of a favorite dish, then perhaps freeze half or more to be thawed at some later time. The United States Department of Agriculture has an excellent pamphlet called "Cooking for One or Two" on the subject of preparing small meals.

The best approach to good nutrition is to practice moderation and variety in our diets, remembering that we will get all the vitamins and minerals we need from a well-balanced diet. While the typical "one-a-day" vitamins will not hurt, we probably don't need to take supplementary vitamins or minerals unless prescribed by a doctor for some specific reason. Finally, (and we may be a bit biased when we say this) we believe one of the best beginnings to good nutrition is the company of good friends—good friends to dine with, to cook with, even to disguise leftovers with.

Medication

Remember, *you* have the final responsibility for your health care, so—unless you become incapacitated—what you put into your body is ultimately *your* decision. But often you may have to seek out and cooperate with medical professionals. In dealing with your doctor (your health advisor), for example, you should keep in mind the following general guidelines for the intelligent use of medications:

1. Feel free to ask your doctor if there is a way your health problem can be treated without drugs.
2. Ask how this medication will help you, and also ask about its side effects.
3. Check with your doctor before you stop taking any medication. If you need to, ask for written directions.
4. Be sure to let your regular doctor know about *all* other medications prescribed for you by other doctors. Include over-the-counter (non-prescription) drugs you are now using.
5. Before an operation, tell your doctor or dentist all the drugs, including alcohol, that you are taking.

Your pharmacist is a specialist in medications. In dealing with the pharmacist you should:

1. Be sure to check whether any new medication is compatible with the other medications you are already taking.
2. Ask if there are any foods or beverages, coffee, alcohol or other drugs which you should avoid

while taking your medicine. Ask whether or not it is safe to drive a car or operate machinery while taking your medication.

3. Ask for easy-to-open (non-childproof) containers.

At home you should:

1. Keep a written record of all medications, including any drug to which you are allergic.
2. Develop a schedule to help you take the correct pill at the correct time.
3. Read the labels of all over-the-counter drugs to become familiar with the contents.
4. Throw away all outdated prescriptions.
5. Seek counseling for problems such as anxiety, nervousness, sleeplessness, loneliness, and boredom. Medication, like alcohol, gives only temporary relief.
6. Go directly to bed after taking sleeping medicine.

Things you should *not* do at home:

1. *Do not* take any more medications than are absolutely necessary. (The more different drugs you take at a time, the greater the chance of adverse effects.)
2. *Do not* take a double dose if you forget to take your medicine at the proper time.
3. *Do not* change the dose or timing of any medication without your doctor's knowledge. If a medication causes adverse effects, notify your doctor *immediately.*
4. *Do not* take any drugs on the advice of friends because your symptoms appear similar to theirs.

5. *Do not* take any drugs in the dark.
6. *Do not* keep drugs on a bedside table. (An emergency drug such as nitroglycerine is an exception.)
7. *Do not* smoke in bed.

Fitness and Flexibility

The physical fitness trend has given birth to innumerable exercise classes, marathon races, and tennis tournaments. While we admire those who can excel in such difficult events, most of us can achieve a satisfactory level of fitness without trying to leap tall buildings in a single bound. But whether people become involved in a program of physical exercise because they are concerned with their appearance or because they have become aware of the importance of physical activity for good health and well-being, most will discover that the more they do, the more they *can* do.

Fitness is not some strange new addition to our lives. Most of today's seniors grew up in an era when walking somewhere was not for exercise: it was transportation. Some people really did walk miles each day just to get to school. Keeping warm often meant shoveling coal or splitting endless cords of stubborn wood. Physical exercise was part of everyday life. But today, with all our modern conveniences, we must reach beyond our normal activities for healthy physical exercise.

Probably the greatest gift the current fitness movement has given to seniors is the easy availability of exercise programs in many community organizations. But we would offer a word of caution: Regardless of your age, when beginning a program of exercise beyond your normal level of activity, have a physical examination and talk with your doctor about how much you can do and how quickly you can progress. Most studies show that regular exercise, along with a reasonable diet and a positive outlook can not only add years to our lives but make those years much more enjoyable.

One of the most common physical changes that comes with aging is a loss of flexibility. To some degree this may be due to arthritis or other health problems, but for many of us this loss comes from an inactive life-style. But for the most part, we can regain that ease of movement with stretching and flexibility exercises like those that follow. Always begin an exercise session by relaxing and warming up both your body and your mind. Don't push yourself too hard in the beginning. Stretch, but not so far as to hurt.

Lie down on your back on a carpeted floor or pad with your legs straight and arms at your sides. Take three deep, slow breaths, and think of something simple and pleasant such as floating in warm water or lying in the sun. Enjoy this for a few minutes. Then check your body for tension. If you find a tense area, tighten your muscles in that area as much as you can for a few seconds and then relax. Continue checking your body and repeat this process until you are completely relaxed. For the next five minutes breathe deeply and slowly, letting all the tensions and problems of the day drift away.

After your quiet time, one good warm-up exercise is the leg lift. Inhale and count to five slowly, as you raise your right leg until it is vertical or as high as you can lift it. Then exhale and slowly lower your leg, again to a count of five. Do the same thing with your left leg. Repeat three times with each leg.

The neck roll is a good exercise to begin your session. It helps to relieve stiffness and tension in the neck and upper shoulder area. Sit cross-legged on the floor or just seat yourself normally in a straight backed chair. Rest your hands on your knees or in your lap. Breathing slowly, drop your head forward, letting your chin rest on your chest. Hold it there while you count to five. Slowly raise your head. Then let it fall slowly toward your back, again as you count to five. Bring your head up once more. Now lower it slowly to your right shoulder, count to five; bring your head back up and lower it to your left shoulder. With a final count to five, lift your head to its normal position. Repeat this entire process three times.

The next two exercises are more difficult but can be worked up to gradually. Remember, "Use it or lose it!"

The forward bend can be as easy or as difficult as you choose to make it. To begin, sit upright on the floor with your legs together and stretched out in front of you. Take a deep breath and stretch both arms up over your head. As you exhale, bend forward trying to touch your forehead to your knees. (Don't be discouraged if you don't touch your knees. Just stretch as far as you can without feeling pain.) Let your arms rest on your legs and relax your neck and shoulders. Hold this position, breathing lightly for a slow count to thirty or as long as you can. Slowly return to the upright position, then lie down on your back and relax.

Our last exercise helps to strengthen the back and firms jaw lines. To begin get down on your hands and knees with your back straight—as much like a table as you can be. Inhale then exhale arching your back, tucking your chin to your chest. Hold for five seconds, then relax and return to the table position. Inhale again and drop your back into a "sway back" position, bringing your head back to look up. Hold this for five seconds, release and again return to the table position. Repeat the exercise three times.

When you have finished your exercise session, take five to ten minutes and repeat the relaxation and tension release process.

For greater activity, even simple exercises such as walking, swimming, bicycling, or canoeing will help to improve muscle tone, flexibility, and lung capacity. Most experts recommend beginning slowly and gradually increasing your schedule. Try to have set times of the day and week for your sessions. This can make it easier to stay on your schedule. Add to the program as you feel comfortable. A good exercise program does not have to stretch you to painful limits. In northern climates during the winter, it may be a good idea to wear a protective mask against the cold when exercising outside. But it is certainly not wise to push yourself to strenuous activity when you are ill or when weather conditions are bad. (And, remember, a daily walk or swim can be more enjoyable in the company of a friend.)

Exercises vary greatly in their intensity and in the demands they make on the body. Generally, exercises that allow steady movement of many muscles and do not involve sudden highly stressful exertion are best. Activities that slowly increase breathing rate will improve lung capacity and heart tone, placing less strain on the heart and circulatory system. Some of these activities are listed below in order from low to high intensity in terms of the sustained movement that is needed to improve heart and lungs.

Low: walking
           skating
           canoeing
Moderate: swimming
           downhill skiing
           bicycling, jogging
High: cross-country skiing
           running

Many others could be added to this list. But of the forms of exercise listed, many sports and health authorities say that swimming has the most benefits and the fewest risks. Walking and bicycling, however, are probably still the most popular forms of exercise. Ironically, the game of golf, often thought of as a good form of exercise, is relatively poor for improving muscle tone or heart and lung capacity. This is partly because it offers little of the sustained movement needed to really improve our physical capacities. However, even the less valuable stop-and-start type exercise such as golf or bowling is a vast improvement over doing nothing. Many people choose walking as one of the best ways to get some exercise and to get around. For those who are able and determined enough, jogging or running might be the next step in a graduated program.

Many of us find it difficult to stay enthusiastic about physical fitness programs when we're exercising alone. One solution is to get involved in one of the many group fitness programs offered in nearly every community. Whether your interest is folk dancing, swimming, walking, or jazzercise, there is probably a group close by that offers it.

To find out exactly where these programs are in your community, check with community education programs, senior citizen clubs, church groups, and both the YWCA and YMCA. Often these organizations will offer activities especially for seniors, but feel free to venture into other groups as well. Another advantage of keeping fit in a group program is that it's a great way to socialize and meet new friends. It's easy to smile at someone when you've worked up a sweat together.

Sexuality

A few things need to be said about sexuality. Because of the many conflicting attitudes about sexuality, it is often a difficult subject to consider and discuss. Conventional "wisdom" also contributes to the difficulty. Many of us, for example, were brought up to believe that after people reach a certain age (which keeps changing!), they are "over the hill" sexually. Some of the cruelest jokes are those which make fun of older persons' sexuality. The "dirty old man" or "old bag" expressions reflect a great deal of ignorance about aging and sexuality. We know that people, if they so choose, can remain active sexually into advanced old age, unless some physical problem interferes. Persons who are disabled or handicapped can still be active sexually. Whether one chooses to be active sexually or not is a matter of individual preference. Many earlier fears and attitudes are changing. In the past, for example, doctors were often afraid to sanction sexual activity for anyone with a heart problem. Now researchers say that even one who has had a heart attack can resume sexual activity after the condition is stabilized. (Persons with heart problems should check with their doctor about this.)

One of the greatest obstacles to remaining sexually active is often simply a lack of a partner. There are far more women than men in the over-sixty bracket. Then, too, many will choose not to be involved sexually for personal reasons. This is perfectly acceptable. In discussing sexuality, our concern is only to let people know that age itself should not be a limiting factor.

If sexual problems are encountered, the first thing a person should do is consult a physician with whom he or she feels comfortable discussing the problem. Some sexual problems, such as impotence in men, can be caused by a physical problem. Most sexual problems, however, result from emotional difficulties. Sometimes, especially in a marriage of many decades, partners can become simply bored with each other. A bit of romance can usually do wonders for any relationship, as we all observed when Archie Bunker took Edith for a second honeymoon trip.

Masturbation is recommended by some physicians for sexually-deprived individuals. And nature attempts to relieve sexual tension via dreams. At any rate, sex is nothing to worry about or feel guilty about. It is not a primary need like food or shelter or intimacy. One can get along without it, but one should be aware that it can enhance life and not try to shun it nor deny its existence.

Finally, it is important to remember that our ability to be sexual is nothing to be embarrassed about or ashamed of. Our sexuality is truly a gift of God, meant, like all gifts, to be enjoyed but used wisely.

Variety

It is certainly true that as we age we experience certain physical changes that make the world seem somewhat duller than it once was. However, a little ingenuity can go a long way in keeping our personal world a bright and interesting place in which to live.

Many of us experience some degree of vision loss with aging, which may cause very subtle colors to look drab. In this event, it might help to change the colors in our homes to brighter shades. A few changes such as brighter pictures on the wall, colorful accent pieces or more brightly colored draperies or walls can help to create this effect without costing a great deal.

Our sense of smell tends to diminish somewhat also, but we can add interesting effects by wearing perfume or aftershave more often and bringing home fresh flowers. Incense is another possibility for adding more sensory stimulation to our lives.

Also, our senior years may be a time when many of us have dietary restrictions, and food may be tasting more bland anyway. This calls for more experimentation with food. It may be true that there are foods we can no longer eat, but there are undoubtedly many other foods which we have never tried. Booklets and pamphlets are now easily available with simple ideas for interesting meals. These helpful booklets (such as "Cooking for One or Two") are available at many community centers, at congregate dining sites, and through the United States Department of Agriculture.

Experimentation is a key word in keeping life interesting. Whenever things seem dull, we have the option to change ourselves or something in our environment. We should be open to trying new things. Life is full of changes, so we might as well take charge and select the ones we know will please us.

Staying Home

Whether it's a little cottage with a garden, a mansion on a lake, or that special apartment we've made our own for the last several years, home in many ways is the center of our lives—the place we belong. Is it any wonder then that in our senior years, when so many things in our lives are changing, home is the last thing we want to give up? But difficulties such as inflation, physical problems, the death of a spouse, or the absence of children who have grown up and moved away can make us feel as though we are under pressure to give up our home. In some cases the move may become necessary. But there are many alternatives to consider before making such a decision.

Support services available in many communities can make it much easier to maintain our independence and our home. For instance, homemaker and chore services can take care of many household cleaning tasks and repair jobs that may be difficult to handle. For a delicious, well-balanced meal and a few hours of socializing with good people, call the nearest site of the Congregate Dining Project. This is a federally-sponsored program and can be found in most neighborhoods nationwide.

Seniors with medical problems may use a home nursing service. These organizations will send a registered or practical nurse to the home to treat health problems or to give medications. They may be listed under "Nurses" or "Home Health Service" in the Yellow Pages.

Many other services may be available depending on your area. Local senior clubs are good places to find out what services there are and where to go or call for information. Some of this help may be free or very inexpensive. But even if the cost is higher, it is usually less expensive for a senior to stay at home by using support services than for that person to have to move to a nursing home.

If it seems time to sell your home, there are some very interesting options in living arrangements. You might want to consider sharing an apartment with a friend. This may provide most of the help you need and pleasant companionship as well. It is also a good way to keep down living costs. Another choice to look into is senior citizen housing. These apartment buildings are built especially with seniors in mind. They have conveniences such as elevators, ramps, and security systems. Most have social rooms for potluck dinners, club meetings, or craft classes. Rubbing elbows with other residents makes it easier to make new friends. Also senior citizen housing is nearly always federally subsidized, so the cost to the resident is low. And you can still enjoy making your own home. However, waiting lists for these apartments are often long, so be sure to put your name in as early as possible if you're interested.

It is really important to remember that whether you continue living in your family home or move elsewhere, you will nearly always have choices about where and how you live. Certainly there may be times when those choices are much more limited than any of us would like, but to exercise that right to choose, even the smaller things in our lives, is one way of maintaining a sense of power. And that is an important part of feeling alive.

Nursing Homes

The Home. One of the most feared and often misunderstood institutions of our time is the nursing home. It is viewed by both seniors and their families with great apprehension. However, some good information can often alleviate these fears.

Although many people view nursing homes as places where most older people will eventually live, the fact is that only a small percentage of people over sixty-five are living in nursing homes. And only one out of every four persons in that age bracket will spend any time in such a home. These facts taken together indicate that most people do not go to nursing homes and that many people who do will eventually return to independent living.

Another important fact is that various levels of care are offered by different types of nursing homes. For Medicaid and Medicare purposes, four classifications have been defined. First, the *skilled nursing home* provides professional nursing care day and night. An *extended care facility* provides this same type of care for people who have just left the hospital and need continued care for the health problem for which they were hospitalized. An *intermediate-care facility-I* provides skilled nursing care also, but only during daytime hours. And the *intermediate-care facility-II* does not provide skilled nursing care; it serves mainly those who have few medical needs. Also, many homes provide more than one level of care for their residents.

When considering a nursing home, there are some important factors to keep in mind. A primary consideration is whether the home and its administration are currently licensed by the state. Location can be important to residents who are mobile and independent, for easy mobility and opportunities to be self-reliant are major elements in regaining or maintaining one's health. If possible, when inspecting a nursing home, it is a good idea to get to know some of the residents, since people make up an important part of the environment. Try to spend some time talking with its residents about the quality of their lives. How is the food? How do they spend their time? Are parties, field trips, and other activities frequently scheduled? How many personal possessions are residents allowed to keep with them? Inquiries such as these can make choosing a nursing home much less of a mystery.

Finances, of course, are an important consideration. Find out from the start what the cost will be and how much of it will be covered by Medicare or Medical Assistance. And it may be a good idea to ask for an itemized bill to check on the cost of extended services. More information about nursing homes is available through local, county, state, and hospital social service departments. Also, many areas have a nursing home patients' advocacy service that can be quite helpful.

A Patient's Bill of Rights

Since almost every one of us at one time or another becomes a patient in a hospital, nursing home, or some other health care facility, we should be aware of our rights as a patient. These rights are not just guidelines but federal laws. Remember that, as a patient, we are hiring someone to work for us. We are an employer, and we have the right to expect the person we hire for our health care to follow all the rules. Following is the Patient's Bill of Rights, Minnesota Statute #144.651, Sessions Laws 1973, Chapter 688.

1. Every patient and resident shall have the right to considerate and respectful care;
2. Every patient can reasonably expect to obtain from his physician or the resident physician of the facility complete and current information concerning his diagnosis, treatment, and prognosis in terms

and language the patient can reasonably be expected to understand. In such cases that it is not medically advisable to give such information to the patient, the information may be made available to the appropriate person on his behalf;

3. Every patient and resident shall have the right to know by name and specialty, if any, the physician responsible for coordination of this care;

4. Every patient and resident shall have the right to every consideration of his privacy and individuality as it relates to his social, religious, and psychological well-being;

5. Every patient and resident shall have the right to respectfulness and privacy as it relates to his medical care program. Case discussion, consultation, examination, and treatment are confidential and should be conducted discreetly;

6. Every patient and resident shall have the right to obtain information as to any relationship of the facility to other health care and related institutions insofar as his care is concerned; and,

7. The patient and resident have the right to expect reasonable continuity of care which shall include, but not be limited to, what appointment times and physicians are available.

Federal and state laws also mandate a list of rights for patients of long-term care such as is offered by nursing homes, convalescent centers, and extended care centers. While these rights include the rights already listed, there are some important additions.

Space does not permit a full listing of these rights. However, some of the most important rights are:

1. A right to full medical information about our medical problems in language we can understand.
2. A right to stay where we are; we cannot be arbitrarily transferred to some other facility without good cause.
3. A right to manage our financial affairs; this includes a quarterly accounting to us and our families, if we so choose.
4. A right to voice our opinion on matters relating to our care and the day-to-day activities of the facility.
5. A right to freedom from any mental and/or physical abuse.
6. A right not to have to perform any kind of work or services for the facility.
7. A right to as many personal possessions and clothing as possible without interfering with the rights of others.
8. A right to meet with any religious, community, or government groups we wish.
9. A right to confidentiality.
10. A right to privacy and dignity. A right to privacy with our spouse. A right to share a room with a spouse unless medically not wise.

Most states have laws designed to protect all consumers of health care. A complete list of patients' rights is available from your State Association of Health Care Facilities.

Death and Dying

Death is a fact of life that American society often denies. It has been suggested that many of our elaborate rituals and procedures surrounding death reflect an unwillingness to look realistically at this part of life. In earlier times, with high infant death rates and many infectious diseases still not under control, most people came to know death as a common visitor. Now it is possible for a person to grow up well into adulthood without ever having had a direct encounter with death. This leaves many older persons in a peculiar and often uncomfortable situation. While no one likes death or enjoys discussing the subject, many older persons are familiar with it. According to a study by the National Institute of Mental Health, most older people have already worked through a kind of acceptance of death. The problem is that often *the families* have not. Even professional people frequently refuse to listen to one's feelings about it.

Dr. Elisabeth Kübler-Ross has worked extensively with dying patients, and she believes that a person goes through definable phases when facing death. First, she states, we go through a *denial* of death. Some may consult several doctors, for example, or refuse to take medications because "there really isn't anything wrong." Most will deny the facts for a short time. The second phase is *anger*—being angry over the circumstances, the timing, and so on. This, again, is quite normal. Thirdly, we tend to get involved in *bargaining*: "It's okay, but only if I can make it until Christmas." In the fourth stage, *depression* sets in as we realize that the inevitable will really happen. Finally we experience *acceptance* and the quiet peace that comes with acceptance. Often, at this stage, a dying person will want to be isolated from most people to allow time to prepare for the end. Families sometimes mistake this for rejection. Dying persons may not go through all the phases, and others may go through them all several times. It is important to remember that we are individuals, and that no two people will have exactly the same way of dying, even as we do not have the same way of living. Most dying persons wish to discuss their situation with others, but some feel uncomfortable bringing it up. It is a great mistake when, on well-meant advice from others, we do not discuss the subject openly with a dying relative. In most cases, open discussion, tempered with hope, is the best medicine possible. Research reveals that most dying patients are well aware of their circumstances. Many even have a deep intuition about how long they will live, often surprising doctors.

Death is a great reality of life. Death limits us on this earth by drawing uncertain borders on our lives. Thus we are called to make each day count in every way. As Vice-President Walter Mondale reminded us, our friend Senator Hubert Humphrey taught us not only how to live, he also taught us how to die.

6

Emotional Power

Feelings

Our emotions or feelings have a great deal of power. We tend to think that certain people or cultures have more or different feelings from those of others. In truth, all peoples of the world experience basically the same feelings; but the kind of behavior that follows a given feeling may vary according to cultural expectations. Remember that emotion is a built-in part of us that warns us, comforts us, and makes life worth living. Feelings in and of themselves are neither good nor bad, but sometimes the things we do with feelings can be destructive. Thus it is all right to feel anger towards someone or something, but it is not right to commit an act of violence against that person.

Many of us were raised in an era where feelings were repressed or denied. We now find ourselves in somewhat the opposite extreme: an age where feelings are often praised above thought. Actually, an excess of thought without emotion is empty; and an excess of feeling without thought can be dangerous! We should seek ways of dealing with our emotions that will provide the necessary release without harming ourselves or others. We know that totally repressed emotions can lead to illnesses, such as gastric ulcers or colitis. In fact, some researchers are now linking cancer with a person's emotional makeup. It is also well known that denying emotion is perhaps the primary cause of most depressions and mental disturbances, and many medical people believe that the repression of feelings may be part of what leads to addiction to alcohol and other drugs.

What are some typical feelings? There are over 140 English words defining feelings. The "basics" are fear, anger, self-pity, loneliness, and joy. If we attempt to repress the "negative" feelings, such as anger or fear, we will also find more difficulty with the "good" feelings such as happiness or joy. Ways that people sometimes avoid feelings are called defenses, and we say that someone is being defensive when he or she is avoiding feelings. Defenses are not bad. They are simply another part of us designed to protect us from harm. Some examples of defenses are denying, changing the subject, humor, blaming, rationalizing or making excuses, and projecting. Sometimes we need to deny a painful event. Many of us, when we first received word of the death of a loved one, said, "No, it can't be." This denial helped us to deal with the shocking and painful nature of the event. So defenses are often helpful. However, if we use defenses all or most of the time, we can lose touch with our feelings and finally with other people, which can be disastrous, both physically and emotionally. Certain times and events in people's lives seem especially related to feelings and how we deal with them. The following will be some examples of these, along with some suggestions as to how we might cope appropriately.

Stress

Stressful situations have long been a favorite topic for every medium from television commercials to classic movies. Who could forget the distress in the eyes of Humphrey Bogart as he said goodbye to Ingrid Bergman in *Casablanca*? But on a more realistic and personal level, stress can be a cause of many serious medical and psychological problems. And since researchers have found some effective ways of dealing with stress, it is important for us to be aware of both the problem and some possible solutions.

In the twentieth century, humankind has invented more ways to cause stress than ever before. Our technology has made the stress in our lives different from what it was even fifty years ago. Many people who witnessed the invention of the automobile have lived to see a man walk on the moon. Changes in science and industry of such gigantic proportions are bound to have a profound effect on our lives. We now must cope with traffic jams, noise, computer errors, environmental pollution, and an inflationary economy. Is it any wonder we find it difficult from time to time?

It is important to remember that our senior years also bring with them certain stressful situations that may be unavoidable. Some of these, such as a loss of income due to retirement, we may predict and prepare for; others, such as the loss of a loved one through death, may take us completely by surprise.

Because stress is so much a part of our lives, and because we can learn to cope with it effectively for better physical and emotional health, we need to be aware of how it works and the effects it can have on our health.

Basically, there are two types of stress. Short-term stress develops in situations that evoke our body's emergency "fight or flight" response. Whenever we rush to meet a deadline, close a high-pressure business deal, or act in an emergency situation—we experience this type of stress. According to Dr. Joel Rauchwerger, research director for the Stress Relief Center in Houston, Texas, people who fill their lives with short-term stress situations have "hard driving" personalities and are very high heart attack risks. These people are often extremely successful in the business world, but they may die of a heart attack before they have the opportunity to enjoy their success. When we live with short-term stress over a long period of time, our bodies are constantly pouring adrenalin into our systems. Although this can help us through a time of emergency, in the long run the body cannot handle continuous experiences of this kind, and the result may be a heart attack.

The other type of stress is long-term stress. It can be described as a chronic and internally waged long-term response. This type of stress develops when we are not dealing with our emotions but trying to hide them away from other people and even from ourselves. Whenever we hold a grudge rather than sharing our anger with the other person, stay in an unhappy marriage without trying to make it better, or feel trapped in a job we do not like but are afraid to leave, we are subjecting ourselves to long-term stress. Again, Dr. Rauchwerger has noted that people who surround themselves with long-term stress may seem easygoing on the surface while they are actually experiencing continual dissatisfaction and repressing such feelings as anger and disappointment. They usually find it difficult to forgive other people and hold many resentments inside. This type of person is apt to become a cancer patient.

The relationship between cancer and long-term stress is not immediately apparent. But according to Dr. George Solomon, chief of psychiatry at Valley Medical Center in Fresno, California, "There is growing evidence that there is natural resistance to cancer in the human body. When the body's immunological system isn't working well, when it is suppressed, cancer can get a stronghold." Long-term emotional stress—especially depression—can weaken a person's immunity system, and this can make the body more susceptible not only to cancer, but to many infectious diseases.

Researchers have also found that the healthiest type of personality for handling stress is the person who does not drive himself or herself hard all the time but can relax when he or she needs to. This person also has learned to deal with emotions by recognizing them, experiencing them, and letting them out *without hurting others.*

What to Do About Stress

What can we do about the stress in our lives and the ways in which we deal with it? The following are four basic steps recommended by stress researchers.

1. Assess your life-style and make the necessary changes.
- Are you a clock watcher? Do you often feel rushed or under pressure?
- Do you often feel dissatisfied, frustrated, or unhappy but conceal these feelings from others?
2. Exercise properly to keep your body healthy and to release some of the tension that stress can create.
3. Try to include B complex and C vitamins in your diet.
- B complex vitamins help the nervous system and help the body to take energy from proteins, fats, and carbohydrates. They can be found in eggs, nuts, whole grains, peas, and beans.
- Vitamin C (ascorbic acid) helps gums and tissues and strengthens the walls of blood vessels. It may also help the body's immunity system. It can be

found in citrus fruits, strawberries, pineapple, broccoli, green pepper, turnip greens, potatoes, and sweet potatoes.

4. Learn to relax.

- Try your own techniques, such as listening to soft music, taking a hot bath, reading, gardening, or whatever helps you to slow down and relax.
- Try structured relaxation techniques such as those listed below.
  - Sit comfortably in a chair or lie down on your back. Put your arms over your head. Tense all the muscles in your body and hold for about 10 seconds. Let go. Begin breathing slowly and deeply, expanding your abdomen as you breathe in to a count of 4. Hold your breath to a count of 4. Breathe out from the top of your lungs down, to a count of 8. Continue this deep breathing for 5 to 10 minutes. Visualize all the tension in your body being breathed out like a cloud from your lungs. Rest.
  - Sit or lie down and breathe deeply and slowly. Beginning with your feet, imagine that a warm glowing feeling is beginning to relax your body. Slowly, let this feeling move up your legs. Soon it begins in your fingertips. It moves up your arms, up your stomach and chest. Finally, it moves to your shoulders, neck, and head. Experience this warm glowing feeling all over and through your body. Picture in your mind's eye a candle flame and quietly watch this candle flicker and glow.

While the first step need be done only occasionally, the last three could be done as a daily activity. Regular relaxation can relieve the minor stresses before they become major problems.

Grief

Since the beginning of time, people have experienced powerful emotions at the loss of a loved one. Human beings will probably always have a difficult time with grief. In earlier periods of our history people seemed to deal with grief in healthier ways than we now see. Perhaps they were more accustomed to death, or perhaps they had more religious and social rituals than we have now. Also, families tend to be more fragmented today, so we often do not find the support that we need.

Most people will have experienced several major losses by the age of sixty-five. There are literally millions of widows and widowers. We lose brothers and sisters, often children, and usually our parents. What younger persons do not understand sometimes is that, although we can often accept the death and even see it as a relief to suffering in a long-term illness, dealing with the end of the relationship is difficult. It is hard to comprehend the million ways in which companionship and closeness can develop in a relationship during half a century of being together. And it is hard to imagine how that can ever end. Yet we know that all relationships have two things in common: They begin, and they end.

Those who study grief, those who work with people having difficulty with the grieving process, and those who have experienced grief all generally agree that "grief-work" is actually a series of steps we take in saying good-bye to someone. Many books and pamphlets on the subject outline a definite list of steps or phases. However, these books miss the obvious point that we do not grieve for one thing and then go on to the next. Actually, most of us are grieving over many different things at once. Therefore, we can be in the first part of grief over one loss and in another stage over an earlier loss. The extent of difficulty we may have will depend in part on the closeness of the person we have lost, the way in which the loss happened, and our own general ability to deal with change. Usually, we grieve in the following manner:

- Deny or avoid the loss. For example, sometimes the survivor will insist that the person's room remain unchanged, as if the person were soon to return.
- Express feelings. Anger, sadness, depression, and even relief can be part of this. Later, guilt and regret and even physical symptoms may occur.
- Experience immobility. Many have reported feeling unable to complete a simple task such as writing a letter or calling a friend.
- Return to hope. After a time, most people begin to return to a more "normal" set of feelings and are able to look forward to things again.

For some, a strong religious involvement has proven helpful at such a time. Unfortunately, for others, this same intense religious attachment serves as a way of denying one of life's greatest realities: death. Certainly a healthy spirituality is one that embraces death as another part of our spiritual journey.

Individuals may vary in their reactions. We may experience the same feelings many times. Often a date of importance, such as the anniversary of the person's death, may trigger the same feelings all over again. Many persons also report having had some sort of experience of the deceased. Some report seeing the person or having a vivid dream; others hear the person's voice; and still others report sensing the person's presence. This is not a sign of mental illness, but more likely an expression of the depth of closeness in the relationship. We probably never completely recover from the loss of someone especially close, but our chances for a normal and happy life are still excellent. Grief can be a great teacher, and often we can learn a good deal from others who have experienced the same feelings. Support groups and counseling are sometimes needed if the reactions to loss go on too long, if there are dramatic physical symptoms, a loss of feelings, continued isolation from friends, self-destructive behavior, or other signs of a serious nature. In any time of trouble such as this, people and activity are at least part of the answer. This may mean almost forcing ourselves to go to activities at first, but the results are well worth it. Statistics show drastically reduced rates of emotional difficulties among senior citizens who are active in clubs and other activities. And certainly we should remember that grief is also an important spiritual experience, so we should feel free to draw upon whatever spiritual help we find acceptable to us.

Fear

We have nothing to fear but fear itself.
—Franklin Delano Roosevelt

Fear, like all the emotions, is a two-sided coin. We need our fears; they protect us from harm. An instinctive fear of a hot stove or a speeding train may keep us alive. Yet at the same time, fear can become a great enemy. It is possible to become literally immobilized by fear. This kind of immobilizing fear can lead to serious emotional and even physical problems. Excessive fears tend to feed upon themselves. We can become so fearful that nothing appears safe or trustworthy. As we become more fearful, we may tend to isolate ourselves from others; and the less contact we have with people, the more likely we are to suspect the motives of others. With increased isolation, we lose the opportunity for what psychologists call "reality testing." A good example of this is what happened to the famous explorer, Admiral Richard E. Byrd, when he stayed in a small shelter alone for months in the frozen Antarctic. Without any direct human contact, he began to lose touch with what was real and what was not real. He survived only through personal fortitude and the radio voices of others. Fear can become a great enemy. Many of us probably know of "old Mrs. So-and-so" who never answers the phone or goes out for any reason. This person has probably become so isolated that all outsiders seem worthy of suspicion. She has crossed the line from the ordinary fears that all of us have into a deeper state of mistrust and panic. She will need help.

Fear is best dealt with through sharing it with another. We all remember the child or grandchild who came thumping to his parents' room to share the bad dream or the *certain fact* that "there's a bear in my room." Then the bear magically went away. The child was "reality testing." For many of us, there may always be some kind of "bear in my room." The only way to chase the bear out is to let someone know about him!

It is important, too, that we accept many of our fears as justifiable. Fear of medical problems, we know, is justified by statistics, which show that over 80% of us will have a chronic medical problem by age sixty-five. Fear of crime is justified by statistics which reveal that older persons are more frequent victims of juvenile crime and "confidence games" than are other groups of citizens. (Interestingly, these sorts of crimes are *not* as common as was once believed.) Fear of loss, both financial and human, is understandable. Fear of loneliness and isolation, too, is quite well grounded. We should be selective in sharing these fears, however, for some, particularly those younger than ourselves, may not be able to empathize or understand. Nothing is more comforting than talking with someone who has "been there" and who knows from firsthand experience what we are going through!

The effective means of dealing with fear are the following: First, identify the fear. Making a list might help sort out our particular fears. Second, determine what steps can be taken. For instance, we may have a fear of vandalism to our home. There may be an inexpensive way to install an outside light of some kind. The police are willing to provide advice. Third, when we have done all we can about the fear, we should "make friends" with it. Many therapists believe that as we make friends with and *accept* our fears, they lose their power over us.

Depression

Out of the depths have I called to thee, O Lord.
—Psalm 130, *NAB*

What is depression, after all? Many of us hear friends saying "She is depressed again" or "This weather is so depressing." We know depression is that, and more. Many of us recall a time of great economic depression, which began in 1929 and was ended only by a world war. During the worst of these years, many people had very little cash, jobs were scarce, and many simply lost hope. We read and recall stories of stock-market investors jumping from buildings after losing all to the economic crash. But the greater calamity was that large numbers of people who never had much to begin with, then had even less. The scars and pain of those years are still felt by many; it is said that some never recovered from those times. It still seems strange, though, that people who survived those hardships and the great hardships that followed, and are now in better times, still carry within themselves those same hopeless and despairing feelings we call depression.

Those feelings that nearly everyone had in the thirties are very similar, then, to the feelings an individual has who is emotionally depressed. Emotional depression can come even in good times, when we could be feeling good. Some people (and, in fact, some families) seem more subject to depression than others, but no one is immune to it. We have been taught to be strong and courageous to the point where we do not always want to admit such feelings for fear of seeming weak or crazy. Now we know that depression is not something to be ashamed of; it can be understood, and it can be treated.

The dictionary defines depression as "low spirits, gloominess, dejection, and sadness" (*Webster's Twentieth Century Unabridged*). Medically, we can talk of depression as a prolonged state of unhappiness or sadness. There are probably two basic kinds of depression. The first is an externally caused or situational depression brought on by some reversal in our lives. This kind of depression will often go away by itself. The second kind of depression is internally caused and may occur even when our lives have never been better. This kind of depression may have at its roots deep feelings of guilt, self-loathing, or some past hurt that remains inside. The first kind of depression may sometimes lead to the second. Also, severe and prolonged illness may result in a depression. At any rate, the second kind of depression should not be taken lightly. Counseling, psychotherapy, medication, and even a hospital stay may be necessary. Since we know that depression causes and aggravates other illnesses, and that deeply depressed people often attempt suicide, depression is a serious problem. The following are some signs of depression:

- Feelings of tiredness or boredom
- Insomnia or a change in sleep patterns
- Feelings of isolation from others
- Physical symptoms: headaches, pains, change in bowel habits, loss of appetite, loss of sexual interest or ability
- A "false front" of nervous laughter or forced smiles
- Sudden outbursts of emotion
- Deep feelings of guilt or loneliness
- Preoccupation with death or suicide

If you notice one or more of the signs mentioned in your own life or in that of someone else, this may indicate a problem. Most depression, fortunately, is of the first kind, and seeing a new play, calling a friend, or receiving a letter might be enough to break it. But to deal with a more serious depression, counseling may be needed. In counseling, the person would explore previous situations, discuss feelings about events both past and present, and attempt to make some changes in outlook and life-style to prevent a recurrence of the problem. Sometimes support groups consisting of persons with the same problem may prove helpful.

Depression is a common and treatable problem. It is, like any other kind of pain, merely a sign that something is not right. It is a message to us which should be heeded. We need not feel embarrassed about being depressed. We can be helpful when friends or relatives are going through this problem. Sometimes just our presence will help, for often a depressed person will see through some false "cheer-up" attempt. There is probably no substitute for a well-meant "How are you?" And, quite often, a quiet empathetic listener is the best possible medicine.

Alcoholism and Other Addictions

You're never too old to recover.
—Senior in A.A.

Alcoholism is an illness that may occur anytime in the life of any person, regardless of age, social background, economic status, and religious or ethnic heritage. It is a primary illness, and not, as heavy drinking may be, a symptom of another problem. It is progressive. Once a person develops alcoholism, she or he will not be able to return to normal or safe use of alcohol or other mood-altering drugs. Alcohol is a dangerous drug, but alcoholism is a treatable disease. That is, it can be arrested, though not cured. Treatment can be effective even if the person appears unwilling to receive help. Untreated alcoholism can be fatal. Death from alcoholism is often preceded by brain damage and insanity, as well as by serious physical problems. The following is a general description of alcoholism in its three phases. Addiction to tranquilizers, sedatives, or sleeping pills follows the same general pattern.

Beginning Symptoms
- Preoccupation with alcohol (or other drug of choice)
- Rapid use (gulping drinks)
- Use at inappropriate times and places
- Sneaking drinks
- Taking increased amounts
- Losing control
- Blacking out (memory loss)
- Making excuses

Middle Symptoms
- Denial
- Blaming others
- Promising to quit
- Self-deception
- Aggression
- Attempting to control drinking
- Family problems
- Sexual problems

- Job and financial problems
- Guilt and remorse
- Hiding bottles, pills
- Physical problems

Final Symptoms
- Deep delusion
- Inner conflict
- Falls, injuries
- Suicide attempts
- Hospitalizations
- Spiritual bankruptcy
- Brain damage
- Insanity
- Death

Anyone who has more than a few of the beginning symptoms is probably dependent on the drug and may need treatment. The usual course of treatment is a stay of several weeks in a treatment center, during which the person is evaluated medically and attends meetings designed to help with the problem. (Others may attend a program that meets on an outpatient basis.) Treatment for alcoholism and dependency on other drugs is usually very successful, especially so when family members take an active part. The follow-up to treatment usually consists of returning to the center for meetings; and all reliable treatment centers expect their clients to attend Alcoholics Anonymous once or more weekly. A.A. is different from treatment in that it is both a program and a fellowship of people who help each other recover. A.A. is not allied with any religious or political groups, nor with any institution. Continuing recovery from alcoholism will ultimately depend more on A.A. attendance and participation than on any other one factor. Families and "concerned persons" attend Al-anon groups, which use the same steps and program to cope with the problems of emotional involvement with an alcoholic. There are many older persons in this area who are active and happy in A.A., and these people are very willing to help others. A.A. is strictly confidential—hence the use of the word "anonymous" in its title. We should remember that even drugs prescribed by a doctor can be habit-forming.

Further information on addiction to alcohol and other drugs is available through local, state, and federal agencies. A.A. is available in most American towns and cities. People who have concerns about alcohol or other drugs can feel free to discuss this in a completely confidential manner at a local counseling center or treatment facility. Many of these places will help evaluate the problem for no charge.

7

Power to Choose

Self-Esteem

Somewhere along the paths of our lives, many of us learned that feeling good about ourselves was somehow prideful. Most of us took this lesson to heart so well that we have difficulty feeling good about ourselves, our bodies, our abilities, or our strengths. Many of us would hesitate if asked to name five good things about ourselves. When we *begin* our lives feeling unaccepting of ourselves, it makes the difficulties of aging more severe.

Certainly to love oneself to the exclusion of all others is not healthy. But we all need to respect, care for, and love ourselves if we are to be capable of offering these gifts to other people. Even the Bible instructs us to love our neighbor as ourself. And to be accepting of ourselves does not mean that we should be deluded enough to believe we are without fault, but rather that we care enough to strive constantly to overcome our faults. If we have weaknesses we cannot change, we can nevertheless become aware of them and still accept them as part of us. A feeling of self-worth comes from being in touch with our own unique powers, our energy, and the many different facets of our lives. Nearly all of us wish to have something to contribute to life or to the people we love. Self-worth is like a light that can shine on the treasures of ourselves, to show us what it is that we have to give.

Assertiveness

An important part of assertiveness is believing in our own powers and rights as human beings. Essentially, what we mean by assertiveness is claiming our legitimate rights, while recognizing the rights of other people. This is sometimes a difficult balance to strike, but it is important that we make the attempt. If we do not claim our rights and have confidence in our abilities, our youth-oriented society may dismiss us as just more "nominees for the rocking chair." Fortunately, in the last decade or so, older people have become more aware of their numbers and their rights. They have been making fair and reasonable demands of government and society in general—demands for better housing, better nutrition, and a better quality of life. Some of these demands are beginning to be met. Even so, it is still important for each of us to learn to be assertive on our own behalf.

As a teacher put it many years ago, we need to "have the courage of our convictions," while recognizing that other people need to do the same. There are several ways we can do this in our day-to-day lives. When we are faced with a problem, we can choose to address the problem rather than avoid it or to attack the person who presents the problem.

We can claim our legitimate rights of others without anger or apology. By doing this, we can establish a pattern of respect for ourselves and others that will be of use in future situations. We have the power to choose our own activities and work for our own goals rather than to hope passively that these things will be done for us. We can deal with anger constructively rather than suppressing it and letting it build into resentment. We can show our respect for ourselves and others by addressing them as equals. We can be confident in our own abilities. And we can make requests of other people, realizing that they have the right to refuse.

In essence, the key to being assertive is respect, first for ourselves, and also for others.

Standing Up for Ourselves

Many of us have been brought up to be agreeable and polite in all situations. While good manners and agreeableness are certainly good traits, we need to be aware that there are people who will knowingly and unknowingly take advantage of this. Unfortunately, older persons are often unsuspecting targets for "con games." How many of us are aware, for example, that if we sign a contract with a door-to-door salesman, we usually have the right to change our minds for three full business days afterwards? How many of us realize that we can appeal a Social Security decision? Do we know how to read those confusing medical statements hospitals send out under

Medicare guidelines? The list could go on and on, so it is very important to check with the nearest senior citizen worker if we feel we have a legitimate complaint. An unscrupulous business or government official may assume that an older person is too frail or too polite to take action. Many seniors are changing this picture! The scope of this book does not allow space to explain the various ways we can help get our due with a business or government agency. But we will include in the following section a most interesting set of guidelines which may bring a smile to many who have tried to get answers from an agency. This list of suggestions is not intended to blame any one person or agency but merely to provide a bit of insight. Above all, we recommend that persons with problems consult someone they know and trust to have a concern for their well-being.

Guidelines for Making Things Happen

There are times in all our lives when we as individuals find ourselves trying to deal with a company, a system, or a bureaucracy in the hope of making something happen. Even those of us who try to avoid such incidents invariably receive a Social Security check for an incorrect amount or find ourselves with some other valid complaint. We can choose to do nothing at these times, but this can be dangerous because it sets a pattern of not exercising our rights.

Very often in such instances, when we must confront the system involved, it helps to have someone go with us who is more experienced in this particular area than we are. The reason for this is that, unfortunately, we are often stereotyped by the systems with which we must deal. For instance, a man will probably have less difficulty dealing with a car mechanic than will a woman. A lawyer will probably have less trouble getting answers about a sales contract than will a retired postal clerk.

There are many reasons for the difficulties we face when we try to solve a problem that involves a bureaucracy of some kind. Often the problem is due to different attitudes within the system. Some people may wish to help you in every way possible while others are concerned with the rules and regulations. In other situations, the system we try to deal with may be so big that we as individuals seem to be little more than numbers on a computer printout.

Following are some suggested strategies which have been used successfully by people trying to make things happen. We hope they can be helpful to you.

- Try to find out how this organization deals with people who have a grievance. Do they give people the runaround? Are they helpful and direct?
- Be patient and persistent. Let the system know that the problem won't just go away.
- Be humorous. Subtle humor can break through a lot of barriers.
- Be ready to back up your arguments with solid facts and figures. This helps to show that the

problem really does exist, not just for you, but for others as well.

- Get newspaper or other kind of media coverage when this is possible. Take the problem to the public if all else fails.
- Use more than one approach and keep the pressure on.
- Be careful to say only things you can support or on which you are willing to follow through.
- Don't discourage action the system might take (such as appointing a committee or gathering information) just because it is not exactly what you had in mind.
- Don't give up. Changes in any system take time.

Financial Resources

The 1920s rang with the notes of "We're in the money. . . ." With the 1930s came "Brother, can you spare a dime?" But in any economy it is a rare senior who does not need to plan and watch his or her finances carefully. Of course there are as many approaches to this subject as there are seniors, but here are some basic ideas to keep in mind.

Social Security is an important part of the income of most seniors. Although it was never intended to be a complete retirement income, it has become just that for many. It is a fund that most of us pay into for many years to provide some security for ourselves and our dependents during retirement or disability.

Social Security is something you have earned. In fact, you need to contribute for a certain length of time and reach a certain age or become disabled before you can draw benefits. And like most government programs, some procedures must be followed before you can receive your benefits. Fortunately, the people at the Social Security office try to make this as easy as possible.

There are several different types of Social Security benefits. Basically these are retirement benefits, survivors' benefits, and disability income. Retirement benefits fall into two categories: early retirement and retirement benefits begun at sixty-five.

You may apply for early retirement benefits if you are sixty-two or older and are planning to retire. These benefits are figured on a lower scale than benefits begun at age sixty-five. Benefits for retirement at sixty-five are based on how long you have contributed to the Social Security fund and how much money you have earned in that time.

When a worker dies, survivors' benefits may go to certain members of the family, such as the worker's spouse or dependent children.

Social Security also provides disability benefits for workers who become sick or injured and cannot work for more than a year.

So with these different types of benefits in mind, you should contact your local Social Security office under the following circumstances:

• You are sixty-two or older and are planning to retire.

- It is three months before your sixty-fifth birthday, and you may or may not plan to retire. (You automatically become eligible for Medicare at sixty-five.)
- A worker in your family dies, and you or another family member may be eligible for survivors' benefits.
- You become sick or injured, and it appears that you will be unable to work for more than a year.

The people we have spoken with in the Social Security office have been most friendly and helpful. They can take most information over the phone and will mail out forms that need to be signed. But if you are approaching sixty-five, please be sure to contact them *three months before* so there will be no delay in receiving your first check or your Medicare Health Insurance card.

Medicare is another program of great importance to seniors. Basically, it is a federal health insurance program for people sixty-five or older, although some disabled people may qualify sooner. Medicare has two separate parts: Part A of Medicare is hospital insurance. It will help to pay costs of inpatient hospital care, inpatient care in a skilled-care nursing home, or home health care. Part B will help with medical expenses such as necessary doctor bills and outpatient hospital services.

There is a great deal more to know about Medicare. It does not pay for all of your medical bills. Some services are not covered at all, and those which are covered are often not paid completely.

Since government regulations for Medicare change, you should contact your Social Security office for current information. They will be happy to send you free information booklets on both Social Security and Medicare. Be prepared.

In addition to federal programs, many seniors have savings, investments, or pension-fund income. If you are experienced in the financial world, you may not need help in managing these funds. But many of us could use some sound professional advice when it comes to planning our finances for retirement. The choosing of a "financial planner" to work with you should be done carefully. You'll want someone experienced with things like tax laws and sound investments. A lawyer or an established insurance agent may be a good choice. Many banks have persons who specialize in this sort of help as well.

When you have chosen an adviser, you may want to look together at insurance programs. It may be wise for you to purchase a health insurance policy that will supplement your Medicare benefits. If you feel you need this, shop around, and read brochures about the policies carefully; you may even wish to call your state insurance commissioner to see if the insurance company and policy you are considering are well recommended.

Another option to consider with your adviser is how to get the best return on the money you have. You might want to look at money market funds, treasury bills, mutual funds, and other investments that can give a fairly high interest rate, or think about the purchase of an annuity which can give you a guaranteed income for a certain length of time or for life. Many of us feel safe with the federal insurance on our passbook savings account, but there are many other ways to use that money and earn a much higher return with very little risk.

Estate Planning

Many seem to avoid or postpone considering the topic of estate planning, but it is an important one that should be addressed. Many older persons will naturally have accumulated some capital in terms of liquid assets, real estate, or personal property. And a will guarantees that your money or property will be distributed as you wish it to be. It need not be an elaborate one, but drawing up a will is an important part of good financial planning for you and your family. Failure to do this could unnecessarily tie up your assets in prolonged court proceedings. A lawyer can help you with this procedure for a modest fee.

If, for some reason, we cannot or do not wish to handle a given *part* of our affairs, we can legally give someone else we trust the "power of attorney" to do this. In a conservatorship, a person legally grants someone control over *most* of his or her affairs. In a guardianship, a person has been declared incompetent through a court proceeding, and in this case, *all* the person's affairs are turned over to someone else. A conservator or guardian must be bonded for the approximate amount of his or her responsibility. None of the above plans sound pleasant, but they are not necessarily negative and at times can solve many problems. Many persons, for example, may grant power of attorney over business or financial holdings while they are out of the country or otherwise unable to care for things. The word "incompetent," used in a guardianship procedure, is a weighty word with deep importance; such a word should not be used or taken lightly.

In all such cases, legal help is advised. Often legal help can be arranged through a legal aid office, or we may consult a legal referral service to find reasonable help. We have the perfect right to shop for a good lawyer if we so choose.

Choosing Retirement Housing

The choices we face when considering where and how we want to live in retirement are vast and varied. There are a few basic options to be examined. Where and how we want to live as seniors depends on our financial situation, our health, the kinds of activities we desire, and the importance of ties to a particular community, region, or climate. Sadly, finances are all too often the main determiner of what sorts of housing we may "choose." Even with very limited finances, we can improve our lot significantly if we plan carefully. Following are some factors to consider and some options to examine.

The first and most important factor is getting good advice. Most public libraries have a number of books that deal with retirement planning and feature sections on retirement housing. Also, many magazines feature articles and other information on the subject. Financial institutions sometimes offer special information and seminars, and many large corporations present seminars on this issue. Also, many seniors have friends and relatives who have already made a choice; sometimes we can learn a great deal from the mistakes and triumphs of others! It is important not to make an impulsive choice based only on an attractive brochure or a good slide-show presentation. Get advice and opinions from many resources before moving on to the next steps in the process.

Next we need to choose a location. An old saying about real estate is, "You can change anything about a house except where it is." We have to decide where we want to be, based on what we want to do, and with whom. Some may have very strong family and community ties, which they do not wish to break. Others, because of those very same ties, may wish to "give themselves space" from these connections by relocating. Another consideration is whether to be in a small town or big city. The wonderful calm of rural life can easily turn into boredom for someone accustomed to ballet, opera, the local chamber orchestra, or major league sports. On the other hand, the excitement of city life with its higher crime rates, great variations in personal life-style, parking problems, and higher air pollution can quickly discourage a transplanted rural person. Then too, a move to a long-awaited Sun Belt area may fade as old friends and familiar changes of season are missing. If possible, try to test a new location by renting for a season or part of a season. At any rate, be very sure of where you want to be before you have committed yourself completely to that area.

The actual kinds of housing available are almost as varied as the locations, and often just as confusing. The popular image of seniors in various manicured retirement communities is still more the exception than the rule. While these communities are attractive, reasonable, and interesting places to live, there are many other options. Once again, price may be an overwhelming factor. There are government rental assistance programs that may help some get into a high-rise or some other form of apartment setting, but changes in funding such as we have observed in the last few years may greatly limit some of these choices. Also, waiting lists for some of these convenient and reasonable buildings are sometimes years long. Many seniors will continue to remain in their present housing, either owned or rented, simply because they are already happy there and well-established in the community. Buying into a condominium, a mobile home, or a retirement center may be a good way to reinvest profits made on the sale of long-owned assets such as a home or other property. We may be able to take advantage of a "once-in-a-lifetime" tax break on the sale of a home. Caution is in order, since a number of disreputable firms and individuals are only too eager to share in the profits we may have gained from a lifetime of frugality. Therefore, a second opinion is advisable when making the final choice about the kind of housing we will live in.

Other choices, such as long-term residence hotels, residence clubs, even boats tied up at rented slips are also worthy of consideration. Whatever the choice, examine your habits now, since they are likely to be the same later. If you truly enjoy keeping up a lawn and a house, a professionally maintained condominium may be frustrating. If you can't wait to get away from all that, however, opt for the most comfortable choice. Certainly many must already have that message, based on the continuing growth of the Sun Belt retirement communities.

The choices and the means of making the choices for housing available to senior citizens, then, are vast. Fewer than one-fourth of us will spend *any* time in that least-desired "choice," the nursing home. With all this in mind, the final factor involved in making choices about where to spend that final third of our lives, the sixty-to-ninety period, is ultimately, in our opinion, the spiritual factor. Recall that we defined spirituality as anything that gives our lives an added sense of meaning and purpose. Our housing choices, then, should be made by asking which choice will give us that greatest sense of meaning and purpose. For some, it will mean the big move to the sun. For others, it will mean finally buying that plug-in heater for the car, so that *this* winter, when it hits twenty below, the car *will definitely* start. Senior citizen housing options are often limited because of a higher level of poverty among seniors. Yet even a situation we feel forced into may, with some creative advice, be filled with the choices that make life continue to be worthwhile.

A Senior's Bill of Rights

The following is a list of rights to which we believe all seniors should be entitled:

- The right to be healthy, to enjoy that health, and the right to the best medical care available.
- The right to make our own decisions and the right to allow others whom we trust to make some decisions for us.
- The right to think clearly and to reminisce; the right to remember, and the right to forget.
- The right to have whatever feeling we happen to have; the right to express our feelings and the right to keep our feelings to ourselves.
- The right to belong and feel included in whatever group we choose; the right to be alone.
- The right to find God in whatever manner and way we wish; the right to worship and the right not to worship.

8

Where to Find It

"Every time I find out where it's at, somebody moves it." The above anonymous expression, no doubt a product of the sixties, reflects a problem we have in suggesting the best resources for a given problem or need. Accordingly, we will suggest some general ideas in each of the areas and leave some room for you to write in the local phone numbers and addresses most suitable.

Emergencies

Write down important emergency numbers such as police, fire department, and the name and number of a close friend or relative. Most phone books list general emergency numbers for police and fire departments. Most fire departments have their own or have access to medical emergency teams. Do not hesitate to place an emergency call for fear you might needlessly bother someone; your taxes are paid to provide emergency help and you have every right to it!

Phone Numbers:

Nutrition

We still think the Congregate Dining program is one of the best things going. This program provides noon meals at local sites such as churches and schools. Your local agency on aging or senior citizen center can give you the locations and times of such programs in your area. Volunteers are often available to provide transportation if needed. Also, some schools allow seniors to participate in their lunch programs. Churches and hospitals and some senior centers often coordinate "Meals on Wheels" programs that home-deliver meals to people when necessary. Finally, many local restaurants offer discounts on special days or at special times. Senior centers and other agencies also offer nutritional counseling, classes, and literature about proper diets, cooking small meals for one or two, and so forth.

Phone Numbers:

Health Care

Some senior centers offer routine health checkups such as blood pressure checks, eye and ear screening, and the like. Some local hospitals and clinics offer special rates and services to seniors. Many agencies now exist which offer home health care in the form of visiting nurses; this kind of care is often enough to remove the need for nursing home or other institutional care. As discussed earlier in the book, we should always remember that *we* hire those who give us health care. Therefore we have the right to be involved in any decisions regarding our health care, and we should feel free to exercise that right.

Phone Numbers:

Housing

Finding good housing and good advice about housing are often difficult tasks. Continued shortage of funding and an increasing scarcity of low-income housing are at least two factors involved. Most agencies on aging and most governmental social service agencies, however, can provide some ideas about the alternatives available. Sometimes special rental assistance programs can be applied even to housing not of the high-rise variety. The best advice we can give is to keep asking; some agencies volunteer little information unless pressed. Be aware, however, that in many areas a waiting list years long is not uncommon.

Phone Numbers:

Legal Services

Legal services can vary greatly in price, depending on the area and the person or firm consulted. Many areas have Legal Aid clinics which provide free or low-cost legal assistance, and most areas have an attorney referral service. Some attorneys advertise "cut-rate" services, which should be carefully examined before making a commitment, since additional fees can often be accrued during a legal action.

Phone Numbers:

Supportive Services

Senior centers and area agencies on aging often coordinate or offer handyman services, homemaker services, and similar kinds of help designed to allow seniors to remain in their homes. Many of these services are free or at very low cost. Also, youth and school groups sometimes have "Rent-a-Kid" services designed as fund-raisers. Many of these services come and go as funding, energy, and ideas permit, but they are certainly worth the effort to investigate. Some unscrupulous contractors and other individuals may offer similar services at exorbitant rates to people who may not be aware of current prices and rates for materials and service. The best approach is to get several estimates for large jobs, and not to allow someone to do unnecessary work.

Phone Numbers:

Self-Help Groups

Self-help groups such as A.A., Al-anon, Overeaters Anonymous, Emotions Anonymous, and other groups designed to help people cope with personal problems can be extremely helpful. More and more professionals refer their clients to these groups to provide ongoing support. Your local phone book almost always features these groups prominently in both yellow and white pages under "A.A.," "Alcoholics Anonymous," or "Intergroup." Also, local mental health clinics, churches, and other agencies often provide space for such groups.

Phone Numbers:

Social Security

All regional Social Security agencies offer an information service, and many agencies present seminars locally for those interested. While the Social Security system is basically the same as when it was first developed, there are constant small changes in benefits and procedures which may require explanation. And yes, if you are mistakenly given a million dollars, you must return it!

Phone Numbers:

Educational Opportunities

Many communities offer countless interesting courses for adults on a wide variety of subjects. Often seniors can audit (attend a course without taking tests or getting credits) courses at a reduced rate or for no cost at all. Check with local schools and colleges and churches for information; it is never too late to learn. Also, many seniors find fulfillment teaching the many skills they have acquired over a lifetime.

Phone Numbers:

Whatever Else

We'll leave space here for any other phone numbers, addresses, ideas, or interesting thoughts you may deem important.

9

Where to Read It

Recommended Reading

Boston Women's Health Book Collective. *Our Bodies, Ourselves.* New York: Simon and Schuster, 1971.

Butler, Robert. *Why Survive? Being Old in America.* New York: Harper and Row, 1975. (This book won a 1976 Pulitzer Prize.)

Butler, Robert and Lewis, Myrna. *Love and Sex After Sixty.* New York: Harper and Row, 1976.

Kübler-Ross, Elisabeth. *Questions and Answers on Death and Dying.* New York: Macmillan, 1969.

Nouwen, Henri J.M. and Gaffney, Walter. *Aging: The Fulfillment of Life.* New York: Doubleday, 1976.

Wegscheider, Don. *If Only My Family Understood Me.* Minneapolis: CompCare Publications, 1979.

Westberg, Granger. *Good Grief.* Philadelphia: Fortress Press, 1971.

Sources

Alcoholics Anonymous. New York: Alcoholics Anonymous World Services, 1976.

Benet, Sula. *How to Live to Be 100.* New York: Dial Press, 1974.

Boeckman, Charles. "You Can Cope with Stress," *Dynamic Years*. March, 1978.

The Book of Common Prayer. New York: Seabury Press, 1976.

Buckley, Joseph, rev. by Schmidt, Henry. *The Retirement Handbook, 6th Edition.* New York: Harper and Row, 1977.

Butler, Robert. *Why Survive? Being Old in America.* New York: Harper and Row, 1975.

Butler, Robert and Lewis, Myrna. *Aging and Mental Health.* St. Louis: C.V. Mosby, 1977.

Butler, Robert and Lewis, Myrna. *Love and Sex After Sixty.* New York: Harper and Row, 1976.

Grollman, Earl, ed. *Concerning Death: A Practical Guide for the Living.* Boston: Beacon Press, 1974.

Jackson, Edgar. *Understanding Grief.* Nashville: Abingdon Press, 1957.

Johnson, Vernon. *I'll Quit Tomorrow.* New York: Harper and Row, 1973.

Rogers, William. *Ye Shall Be Comforted.* Philadelphia: Westminster Press, 1950.

Rossman, Isadore. *Clinical Geriatrics.* Philadelphia: J.B. Lippincott Company, 1971.

Sheehy, Gail. *Passages: Predictable Crises in Adult Life.* New York: E.P. Dutton and Co., 1976.

Social Security Administration. *Your Social Security.* U.S. Government Printing Office, 1981.

U.S. Department of Health, Education and Welfare. *Social Security Handbook.* 1974.

Wegscheider, Don. *If Only My Family Understood Me.* Minneapolis: CompCare Publications, 1979.

Westberg, Granger. *Good Grief.* Philadelphia: Fortress Press, 1971.

Woodall's 1981 Sunbelt Retirement Directory. Highland Park, Ill.: Woodall Publishing Co., 1981.

Conclusion

The following poem is inspired by an ancient Greek hymn, the *Phos Hilaron* or "Gladsome Light." This song is often used at an evening or vesper service. The idea is that the most beautiful light of the entire day is that soft glow that beautifies the world at day's end. So it is, we think, with human beings. We give off our most lovely light last, in our senior years. A life well-lived and filled with the wisdom, understanding, and tolerance that only experience can bring has a great potential to shine softly on harsh landscapes, thus tinting them more gently with the special glow of evening.

Lights

O gracious light
Pure brightness shining,
In heaven, shine, the gracious glorious light
Of love shining

Now as we come to the setting of this sun
We need to remember
That the sun in its rising up
Or in its going down
Shines just as brightly

And the music of the sun's colors
Dawn or dusk, sings the same beauty

Our eyes this vesper light behold
And sense at once the sure and certain hope
Of a greater, returning day
A day brightened by you and made glorious in
    our hope
To shine some day as brightly
As you shine for us this day

—John Baudhuin

As we end our written words to you, we know
we will not end the flow of knowledge, feelings, and
love that we find wherever we meet senior citizens.
We hope something within these pages will help you
in some way in shaping your life. If so, then our
writing, typing, scratching, and scrawling has been
worthwhile. Peace!

—John Baudhuin and Linda Hawks